# AN INTRODUCTION TO THE GRASS S

(including bam and

D

# AN INTRODUCTION TO
# THE GRASSES

(including bamboos and cereals)

G. P. Chapman, *Bsc., PhD., F.L.S.*
W. E. Peat, *BSc., PhD.*

*Department of Biochemistry and Biological Sciences*
*Wye College*
*University of London*

C·A·B International

C·A·B International        Tel: Wallingford (0491) 32111
Wallingford               Telex: 847964 (COMAGG G)
Oxon OX10 8DE             Telecom Gold/Dialcom: 84: CAU001
UK                       Fax: (0491) 33508

A catalogue record for this book is available from the British Library

ISBN 0 85198 803 2


Printed and bound in the UK by Redwood Press Ltd., Melksham

# Contents

# Preface

Traditionally, when dealing with the grass family, Faculties and Colleges of Agriculture have concentrated on the major cereals and relatively few forage grasses. This approach needs thorough revision for several reasons. Other grasses have become important including those used to stabilise desertified areas, to prevent erosion in the wet tropics and to rehabilitate salinised or otherwise damaged soil. To these can be added the bamboos, conspicuously a renewable resource and one group among many grasses now used for amenity planting.

Changing patterns in education mean increasingly that students from one country study in another and institutions that cannot respond but continue to offer only the customary course content are not only open to a charge of parochialism but are also missing the absorbing challenge of a global view. Who, for example, based in Western Europe could fail to recognise that, increasingly, the real problems in agriculture lie elsewhere?

Not only do we need to take note of an increasing number of species, we have to recognise that grass science has changed and expanded. In the last 25 years grass taxonomy has become more sophisticated and our awareness of photosynthesis in grasses has had radically to be revised. A text book on grasses, therefore, for several reasons is recognisably now a new venture and one that will depart from its predecessors.

Most students initially bring little awareness of grass structures and how these might relate to function. We have therefore attempted in this book to take almost nothing for granted. One feature, for example, of this book is the Glossary to which is prefixed the word 'Critical'. Terms used in agrostology are sometimes peculiar to grasses or, when applied there, depart from customary botanical usage. An attempt has been made, therefore, not only to define the various terms but to highlight the problems they raise.

It is necessary to have a sense of perspective. Amid the preoccupation with the minutiae of glumes, lemmas and lodicules we must recognise that in a hungry world grasses are the centrepiece of agriculture and when we look at one damaged environment after another, grasses offer us some of the best hopes for rehabilitation.

In the drier tropics and subtropics, apart from an obvious concern with cereals, attitudes have changed with regard to range management. Important though this remains emphases are changing and ecology, genetics and physiology increasingly are required to understand and manage such fragile environments.

Grasses form a highly evolved and globally successful family that has drawn the scientific commitment of many specialists. In writing this book our aims have been to elucidate the essentials of grass biology and to indicate where absorbing questions arise whether new or old. This book introduces the grasses. For this size it cannot be comprehensive and so, too, it introduces recent and more specialised grass texts.


G.P. Chapman and W.E. Peat
Wye College
June 1992

# Acknowledgements

Our thanks are due to Malcolm Kernick who read the book in draft and made numerous helpful suggestions, to Jeff Brooks for photographic and artistic help and to Mrs. Sue Briant and Mrs. Margaret Critchley for typing and secretarial skills throughout. We are grateful to Longman Group UK Limited for permission to include Figure 1.1; to P. W. Hattersley of the Biological Resources Study, Australian National University, Canberra and to Cambridge University Press for permission to reproduce Figures 6.3, 6.5, 6.6 and 6.7; to Stephen Renvoize and the Royal Botanic Gardens, Kew for Figure 6.4 and to Miss N. Busri, Wye College, for Figures 7.1 and 7.2.

# Chapter 1

# The Grass Family

Grasses are the world's most important agricultural plants. They include cereals, forage grasses for farm animals, sugar cane an industrial raw material, bamboos which have a multitude of uses, grasses that stabilise various environments, a large group used for brooms, mats and thatching, a large group of ornamental grasses used in horticulture and those that provide lawns, public parks and various kinds of sports turfs. Superficial inspection of grasses can cause them to seem both simple and uniform.

### The 'simplicity' of grasses

With their seeming uniformity, small green flowers and world-wide distribution, grasses often give the appearance of simplicity. 'Simplicity', however, can mean either primitive naïveté or an art-full simplicity that conceals art. For example, cartoonists in a few lines enliven our newspapers in ways that both convey messages and provoke humour. Even more remarkably, what they did yesterday and today they will do tomorrow with unfailing inventiveness. How much does the simplicity of the cartoon reveal and, more interesting, how much does it conceal?

The Poaceae is a plant family that has incorporated much evolutionary innovation whilst shedding much that is superfluous. Its representatives provide models of unobtrusive efficiency whether in rain forest, savanna, circumpolar fringes of vegetation or in responding to the requirements of agriculture and amenity. Grasses clothe our mountains and green the deserts: both those of nature and those of our own making we call suburbs.

## Origins of the Grass Family

**Evidence from distribution.** A commonplace assumption is that the world's land masses now spread out across the globe were originally concentrated in one huge area referred to as Pangea. Figure 1.1 shows in simplified form how, through time, the original land mass is thought to have fragmented. An essential

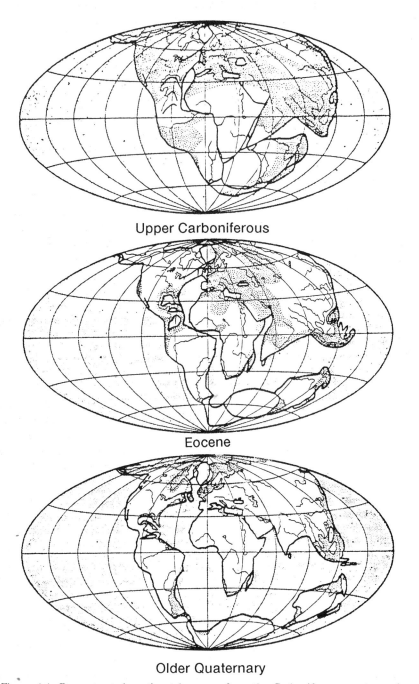

**Upper Carboniferous**

**Eocene**

**Older Quaternary**

Figure 1.1. Reconstructed continental masses from the Carboniferous era to modern times, showing the break up of Pangea (Good, 1964, redrawn from Wegener, 1924).

point to understand is that any recognisable plant group which had evolved and spread across the original land mass might occur on its fragmented parts. Any plant group evolving after the fragmentation would perhaps both have arisen later and been more confined in its distribution.

The grass family apparently evolved early enough to be represented on all the major land masses since the Poaceae is, conspicuously, a world-wide family. If we examine its major subdivisions - the five subfamilies, these are world-wide. When however the various genera are examined, their distribution is seen to be more restricted, prompting the fairly obvious conclusion that many of them probably evolved after the major features of continental separation became established.

Such an obvious seeming conclusion needs further scrutiny to make the point that some genera evolved from others. Again, if a genus has a restricted distribution does it mean that the genus is relatively young, or is it poorly adapted and unable to spread or is it very old but of restricted distribution because it is now uncompetitive? In practice, the study of distribution can shed some light on grass origins provided the data are scrutinized sufficiently critically.

**Timing and environmental change**. Flowering plants, judged by the available fossil evidence, are unknown before the Cretaceous and at its conclusion many familiar plant families are in evidence. From the end of the Cretaceous to the present day (about 70 million years) the flowering plants have diversified. They have done so against a background of considerable climatic fluctuation. The present marked gradation from cold polar to hot equatorial regions has not existed indefinitely to the same extent and, furthermore, the larger plant families predate by many millions of years the major mountain systems on which they are found growing such as the Andes, Rocky Mountains, Alps and Himalayas which are themselves the later results of continental drift. The origin of such mountain ranges should be recognised as offering a new collection of ecological niches to already long existent plant families and which further diversified as a result.

**Grass fossils**. When attention is concentrated upon grass fossils the evidence is 'unsatisfactory'. Such evidence as does exist reveals grasses millions of years old but not dissimilar from present day species. These include equivalents or near equivalents of *Festuca, Nassella, Panicum, Setaria* and *Stipa* in Tertiary times. Of grasses antecedent to these we have no fossil evidence of any convincing kind. There has therefore developed a quite different approach which will now be outlined.

**A phylogenetic view of present day grasses**. Among monocotyledons one theme is conspicuous, namely, the parts of flowers arranged in threes or 'trimery'. A lily for example will have six petals, and six anthers each in two whorls of three and at the centre of the flower will be an ovary consisting of three carpels. So widespread is this theme that departures from it could be interpreted either as preceding it or deriving from it. What makes bamboo flowers especially interesting here is that they are intermediate between a trimerous arrangement and most other grasses, a topic considered in Chapters 3 and 4.

A wealth of other evidence suggests that grasses are a highly adapted and by no means primitive group of plants and so the idea has developed that some kind of bamboo, a 'protobamboo' provided a link with other monocotyledons and was ancestral to modern bamboos and all other grasses. If this idea is adopted an important, and so far unresolved, difficulty arises which concerns the woody and sometimes massive nature of bamboo stems, clearly an adaptation to the forest ecosystem. The dilemma is that while in floral terms bamboos seem relatively 'primitive' their stems suggest a 'derived' or 'advanced' specialisation. We cannot therefore automatically assume that bamboos are primitive and indeed Renvoize and Clayton (1992) regard another subfamily the Arundinoideae as 'the descendant of an ancestral line closest to the earliest grasses'.

Suppose therefore that, for the present, we suspend judgement about which group is the most primitive or ancestral and instead record systematically the features of existing grasses. Eventually it becomes apparent that some features are common to all grasses and some features or groups of features are shared by relatively fewer grasses. We could, if we wished, then refer to them only in terms of similarity or dissimilarity and no evolutionary conclusions need be drawn. We do have however an itch to see things in an evolutionary way and almost unthinkingly read similarity as 'relationship'. From there it is a largely automatic step to suggest lines of descent and, of course, the need to propose some ancestral group resurfaces. See Renvoize and Clayton (1992) for a fuller discussion and Chapter 6 of this present book where certain taxonomic implications are examined.

## Emergence of the Grass Family

While the origins of the grass family remain obscure, the world-wide distribution and importance of the Poaceae are clearly evident. An instructive comparison can be made with another very large and conspicuous monocotyledon family the Orchidaceae. Orchids in general occur in stable habitats and a conspicuous feature today is ecological destabilisation. Tropical forest is being destroyed, towns enlarged, coastlands disturbed for tourism and industry and of course new highways are being laid on an immense scale. Virtually everywhere orchids, through habitat disruption, are in retreat and grasses, the vigorous colonists of disturbed environments, are advancing. Whether it is in new ploughed fields planted with cereals or some plot of land kept clear for football or the freshly planted embankments of a new road, the grasses are so often conspicuous while orchids increasingly become the concern of the conservationist. Were humankind to over reach itself and decline, provided the planet could still support plant growth probably the forest cover would return and create those shady habitats within which epiphytic orchids could re-establish while in drier areas and along forest margins terrestrial orchids might again begin to flourish. For the foreseeable future, though, circumstances favour the grasses and their importance seems likely only to increase. Since humankind and grasses have so close an interdependence this relationship needs to be examined more closely.

## Interdependence

Chaloner (1984) presented a lighthearted, though instructive, allegory that identified dependence of humankind with cereals and in which it was the cereals that took the initiative. We do however believe that hunter gatherers in Neolithic times invented settled agriculture and ultimately this made possible urban societies with an assured food supply within which our modern civilisation began to develop. In Chapter 8 'Domestication' is examined in more detail. Suffice, for the present, to say that wheat, maize and rice, the major cereals, together with barley, sorghum and pearl millet and a host of minor cereals and forage grasses provide the chief component of human diet and much of the feedstuff supplied to farm animals. How certain wild grasses came to dominate world agriculture is not readily explained but it is worth remarking that the choices made by Neolithic farmers about which were the preferred crops have tended to remain of primary importance. What then are the characteristics of grasses and what makes them especially suited to human needs?

## Features of the Grass Life Cycle

If soil is disturbed and subsequently left grasses are often among the first colonists. In a wet environment if temperatures are sufficiently high and nutrients adequate the grass will eventually be out-competed by the emerging shrub and tree flora. In drier habitats where trees establish only very slowly the environment remains relatively open and perennial grasses will maintain a permanent occupancy although they do give way progressively in certain cold and warm deserts to shrubs. If the area is repeatedly disturbed by erosion, deposition or ploughing there is a recognisable advantage to a shorter life cycle - annual or even ephemeral.

Given these alternative considerations certain features of grasses seem to comprise the ingredients of success. A grass 'seed' (defined more fully later) contains both a generous food reserve and a relatively elaborate embryo. At germination therefore it has a 'running start'. A further consideration is that the plant subsequently established is, except for the bamboos, seldom woody or highly elaborate so that onset of the reproductive phase is not delayed and development is readily completed.

Both annual and perennial, grasses are furnished with numerous growth points and these, whether they develop into rhizomes, stolons, tillers or branches, generate a highly competitive growth habit. There is a further aspect of grasses that helps explain their competitive success. They are remarkably drought tolerant a fact which is readily observed in suburban lawns where in prolonged hot summers they brown off but seldom die and rapidly regreen with the onset of rain. Other grasses, too, including our cereals resist drought though in prolonged drought they will suffer some reduction of yield.

This then outlines the importance and the interest of the grass family and in the chapters that follow ingredients of grass biology are more fully examined.

# Chapter 2

# Vegetative Development and Diversity

Since grasses are found in a wide diversity of habitats they show a considerable measure of ecological adaptation. Even so the grass plant is something of an 'all purpose' structure so that the descriptive morphology of growth habit and the progress of the life cycle conforms to a widely recognisable pattern. An exception is the conspicuous woody stem of the bamboo plant but when its anatomy is carefully studied the difference appears more of degree than kind.

## The Grass 'Seed'

The agricultural 'seed' of a grass is actually a fruit. It is a one-seeded, non-dehiscent fruit termed a caryopsis (Figure 2.1). The caryopsis contains the true seed, which in a typical grass has a relatively elaborate embryo situated at one end of the fruit next to a generous supply of endosperm. The relative proportions of embryo and endosperm vary among the grass subfamilies. The grass fruit can vary enormously in size. Those of *Eragrostis tef* are so small that two or three could be put on a pin head. At the other extreme *Melocanna*, a bamboo, has fruits which are many thousands times larger being up to 12 cm long. In rare circumstances, such as *Sporobolus*, the true seed and the caryopsis may be separated.

Figure 2.1. The grains of cereal species: a,b naked grains (a, maize; b, wheat); c,d hulled grains (c, barley; d, oats).

Figure 2.2. A germinating wheat seedling. Three seminal roots have emerged, well supplied with root hairs, and the coleoptile is beginning to elongate. The flaps of tissue between the coleoptile and the roots are the epiblast (uppermost) and the ruptured coleorhiza.

The caryopsis alone forms the grain of the so-called 'naked-grain' cereals such as wheat or maize. In most grasses, however, the caryopsis is retained within accessory structures which have a protective and distributive role and are described later.

The embryo contains the single cotyledon or scutellum, a large elliptical structure appressed to the endosperm. The embryonic shoot and root axes are found at the centre of the scutellum. Depending on species, a small scale of tissue, the epiblast may also be present on the outside of the embryo. When germination begins, the developing shoot expands within a protective modifed leaf, the coleoptile, which splits through the caryopsis. Similarly, the primary root pushes through its protective organ, the coleorhiza (Figure 2.2).

## Vegetative Growth: Leaves

As the plant develops the shoot (or culm) becomes conspicuous. At this stage it consists solely of a series of concentric leaves, with the oldest on the outside, and younger ones forming in the centre, pushing upwards until they finally emerge. The resulting structure of a typical vegetative grass is shown in Figure 2.3.

As the seedling develops, the emerging leaves show variations in structure which are most important for species identification. The mature leaf blade is sometimes very narrow: little wider than its thickness, producing a hair-like or setaceous appearance. In most species, however, the blade is flat or capable of being flattened (laminate). The many species with folded or rolled leaf blades fall into this latter group. Some (mainly tropical) grasses have very stiff setaceous leaves, referred to as needle-like or acicular.

In species with laminate leaves, the arrangement of the young leaf before it emerges through the surrounding leaf sheath is important: whether it is rolled or whether it is merely folded at its midrib. The most important variation in leaf sheaths is whether they possess free margins which overlap or whether the mar-

Figure 2.3. A young vegetative grass plant. The main shoot is on the right, with four leaves visible. The first tiller is shown on the left (with its subtending leaf removed) and has two leaves visible.

gins are fused to form a complete tube.

Leaves may be variously modified, most commonly by being reduced to scale leaves, as readily seen on bamboo culms or on rhizomes (see below), or may be abbreviated to modified sheaths such as the husks surrounding the ear of maize.

The ligule is one of the most important diagnostic features of grass leaves (Figure 2.4a). It is always present, but its texture, size and shape vary widely. Most commonly it is a membranous structure, but this can become stiffened to a scale, or reduced to a fringe of hairs. In bamboos, especially, there are occasional instances of ligules being produced on both the adaxial (inner/upper) and abaxial

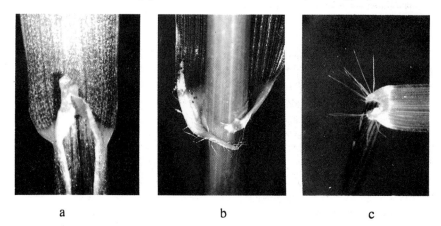

        a                         b                        c

Figure 2.4. Some of the variation of structures at the juction of the leaf sheath and the leaf blade: a) the membranous ligule of *Avena fatua*; b) the auricle of *Triticum aestivum*; c) the oral setae of *Phragmites australis*.

(outer/lower) leaf surfaces. The phenomenon is known to occur, though very rarely, in other species.

Separate from the ligule, the leaves of some species have 'auricles' - ear-like projections also at the junction of leaf sheath and lamina, as in wheat and rice (Figure 2.4b). Alternatively, there may be tufts of hairs in this position known as oral setae, as in *Eragrostis* and *Phragmites* (Figure 2.4c).

## Stems

Successive leaves are initiated by the stem apex, which in most species remains short during vegetative development so that leaves arise close together. The majority of species delay stem development until shortly before flowering, with the exceptions of most members of the Bambusoideae and some other species. When stem development does occur, the structure is fairly uniform: long and narrow with either solid or hollow internodes separated by solid nodes (Figure 2.5). The nodes are usually visible as slight swellings of the stem, but in some cases, notably tropical species the node may be so enlarged as to form a pulvinus.

The anatomy of the mature grass stem is superficially simple, with longitudinal vascular bundles embedded in parenchymatous ground tissue. In species with solid stems. such as those of *Zea* and *Saccharum*, the central parenchyma provides a large store for carbohydrates, which may be later used during seed development.

In species with hollow stems (Figure 2.6a), the vascular bundles are arranged in one or two concentric rings. Where stems are solid, however, the bundles can be more widely distributed although usually more concentrated towards the outside. Columns of strengthening sclerenchyma develop in close proximity

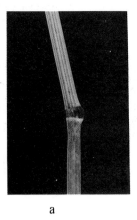
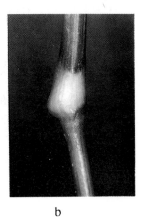

a                                          b

Figure 2.5. External stem structure showing  a) the conventional node of *Bromus sterilis* and b) the swollen pulvinus of *Digitaria exilis*.

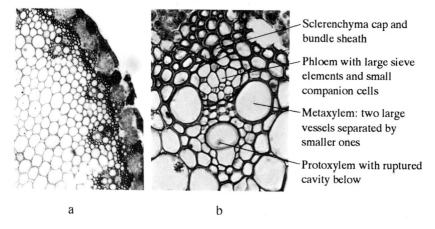

Sclerenchyma cap and bundle sheath

Phloem with large sieve elements and small companion cells

Metaxylem: two large vessels separated by smaller ones

Protoxylem with ruptured cavity below

a                                    b

Figure 2.6. Anatomy of the stem in cross-section: a) part of a wheat internode ($\times$ 56) showing rings of alternating large and small vascular bundles embedded in parenchyma, with blocks of thickened cells (darkly stained cell walls) and photosynthetic cells (dense contents) towards the outside; b) a single vascular bundle from a wheat stem ($\times$350) with the details labelled.

to the vascular bundles. In extreme cases, such as bamboos, the whole of the ground tissue eventually becomes lignified. hence their use for implements, furniture and scaffolding (Figure 2.7).

The vascular bundles in both stems and leaves have a very characteristic appearance in cross-section (Figure 2.6b) with two very large metaxylem vessels outside a row of smaller metaxylem. Phloem is found on the abaxial side of the metaxylem, and often shows a clear distinction between sieve elements and companion cells. A cavity on the adaxial side of the metaxylem is usually found in place of the expected protoxylem. The whole bundle may be surrounded by a variously specialised bundle sheath, which is of major significance for the photosynthetic specialisation in leaves and is discussed in more detail in Chapter 6.

a                                    b

Figure 2.7. Examples of uses of bamboo: a) large scale scaffolding for building construction; b) bamboo veneer used in furniture manufacture.

Vascular bundles pass downwards from a leaf lamina through the sheath to the node of attachment and into the lower internode of the stem. The remaining tissues of both stem and leaves, however, develop and mature from the tip downwards, so that at some stage of development an organ will have maturing tissues, with well differentiated vascular bundles set above a region in which cell elongation is still occurring and where the vascular tissue is only beginning to appear. The consequence is that the earliest xylem cells to differentiate: the protoxylem, do so whilst the cells around them are still elongating. Since differentiated xylem cells have lost the ability to elongate, they are pulled apart, leaving the characteristic protoxylem cavity.

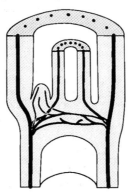

Figure 2.8. A diagrammatic representation of the vascular system at a grass node. Only a small proportion of the whole system is depicted. Adapted from Hitch and Sharman (1971) and Patrick (1972).

An individual vascular bundle can be traced downwards through a leaf and into the stem where it passes through two internodes before finally anastomosing with other bundles. All such anastomoses occur at nodes, in association with other complex junctions and cross-linkages. Vascular branches pass from the stem to axillary buds and/or adventitious roots (Figure 2.8). A particular feature to note is that the cross-linking of vascular bundles at the node provides the possibility for assimilate movement across the plant, and between leaves. The overall strength of an elongated stem depends on the cross-bracing the solid nodes provide. Vascular traces entering an axillary bud are derived both from the subtending leaf and from bundles on the opposite side of the stem, connecting the bud to leaves above and below the subtending node.

Vascular bundles vary in size. The central bundle of a leaf is largest, particularly in species with a well defined midrib. On either side of the central bundle is an alternating series of larger and smaller bundles. In both leaves and stems, strengthening columns of sclerenchyma cells are often found close to, and sometimes connecting with the larger bundles (see Figures 6.3 to 6.7).

The consequence of individual bundles passing from a leaf through two internodes before anastomosis is that an internode will contain approximately twice as many bundles as a leaf. These values are, of course, not constant, and are largely related to the absolute size of the organ. The number of bundles tends to increase as the plant ages and individual leaves become larger.

## Roots

The seminal root system consists of a primary root and a small number (between two and seven) of first order branches. As mentioned earlier, this root system is progressively replaced by adventitious roots which arise at stem nodes and push out through the subtending leaf sheath. Adventitious roots develop from the leaf bases, and eventually replace the seminal roots which grew from the initial seedling.

The anatomy of grass roots is very similar to that of other monocotyledons (Figure 2.9). Within the stele, numerous groups of procambial cells differentiate into alternating strands of protoxylem or protophloem. Large metaxylem vessels eventually differentiate inside the protoxylem. The number of protoxylem poles and metaxylem vessels is largely dependent on root size, so that in the finer roots of many species there is only a single central metaxylem cell. Among the larger roots, there are, however, some consistent differences of taxonomic value. Goller (1983) described the typical pooid root of Figure 2.9 as having a cortex with three-cornered cell junctions and a relatively wide outer cortex of thickened, lignified cells. The stele typically has 10-12 metaxylem vessels embedded in slightly thickened ground tissue. In typical panicoid roots, the cortex is more reg-

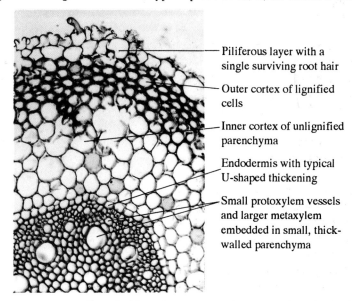

Piliferous layer with a single surviving root hair

Outer cortex of lignified cells

Inner cortex of unlignified parenchyma

Endodermis with typical U-shaped thickening

Small protoxylem vessels and larger metaxylem embedded in small, thick-walled parenchyma

Figure 2.9. Transverse section through a mature wheat root (×92).

ular with four-cornered air spaces and no thickened outer cortex. The stele is larger, with more metaxylem cells embedded in small, thickened tissue, the whole surrounding a thin-walled pith.

## Branching and Vegetative Reproduction

Tillers, or lateral shoots, arise in the axils of the first formed leaves on a shoot. Where these are retained within the surrounding leaf sheath, tillering is referred to as intravaginal, and produces the familiar tufted or caespitose growth habit (Figure 2.10a). Intravaginal tillers develop similarly to the main stem: in species where the vegetative plant shows no stem elongation, the tillers also consist of a succession of leaves laid down around a non-extending stem apex. Grazing animals by preventing further growth of existing tillers can induce the formation of new ones.

a                                              b

c                                              d

Figure 2.10. Alternative growth habits. a) tufted or caespitose development of *Festuca pratensis*; b) the rhizomatous habit of *Elymus repens* with undeveloped scale leaves on the rhizome and upright shoots developing from their axillary buds; c) the surface-spreading stoloniferous growth of *Poa trivialis*; d) 'branch complements' of bamboo.

An alternative form of tillering is termed extravaginal, and occurs where the lateral stem does elongate, and bursts through the side of the surrounding leaf sheath to produce a spreading growth habit. Extravaginal tillers form either rhizomes (horizontally spreading stems which bear scale leaves only: Figure 2.10b) or stolons (the above ground equivalent, which possess fully developed leaves: Figure 2.10c). Both forms then root and produce new shoots at the nodes, permitting a single plant to spread over a wide region.

In stoloniferous species, the distinction between a horizontally spreading stem and a vertically growing shoot is often rather vague, so that a fallen upright stem might root at the nodes and permit vegetative spreading, whilst a horizontal stem may (particularly if it becomes reproductive) turns upwards.

Rhizomatous species (particularly bamboos) are similarly distinguished by their type of branching. In monopodial growth, the apical meristem of the rhizome continues horizontal development, and lateral buds give rise to aerial shoots. In sympodial growth, the apical meristem turns upwards, and an axillary bud continues rhizome growth. In bamboos the aerial stems can produce clusters of small branches at a node – the 'branch complements' – and are characteristic of particular genera (Figure 2.10d).

Figure 2.11. Sand dunes stabilised by a mixture of *Ammophila arenaria* and *Elytrigia juncea*.

In some weedy grasses, the underground development of a complex mass of monopodial or sympodial rhizomes can make eradication very difficult: couch grass (*Elymus repens*) and some bamboos are notorious examples. On the other hand, situations where soil stabilisation is necessary can utilise this growth habit. In habitats of shifting soils, where the grass is liable to become buried, genera such as *Vetiveria* used to create contoured terraces and *Ammophila* found on coastal sand dunes can progressively substitute higher nodes as the effective stem base as the soil or sand accumulates (Figure 2.11).

Tiller, rhizome and stolon growth can all lead to vegetative reproduction. Curiously, through various forms of seed reproduction, the distinction between vegetative and sexual reproduction is blurred: see Chapter 7.

## The Maturing Plant

Throughout vegetative growth, the apical meristem of the stem remains close to ground level and initiates new leaves. Eventually, however, reproductive development begins. The apex increases its growth rate, and initiates the inflorescence whilst the condensed internodes underneath the meristematic region begin to elongate, so that the inflorescence is pushed upwards and eventually emerges from within the enclosing leaves, carried on the main stem or rachis.

The switch to flowering is usually permanent, so far as any single stem is concerned. There are exceptions, however, and a reversion from reproductive back to vegetative development can cause such peculiarities as prolifery (Figure 2.12). Many grasses flower and seed during their first year of growth, but reproductive growth may also be long delayed - exceptionally for as much as a century in some bamboos.

Figure 2.12. Prolifery in *Festuca ovina*. Development of branched inflorescence began, but was interrupted and reverted to vegetative growth. Expansion of potentially floral structures into foliage shoots produced the highly branched structure shown.

Even where flower formation occurs, it is not always particularly effective. *Phragmites australis* flowers readily each year in the British Isles, but seedling establishment seems relatively rare. Not surprisingly, at the climatic extremes for any species, a seedling may develop and persist, but only in the vegetative state, being unable to reproduce sexually. Failure to produce seed can delay or postpone indefinitely the senescence of the vegetative parts of the plant. Apart from these exceptional situations, the switch from vegetative to reproductive growth normally occurs at some point in the life cycle of all grasses, and to this topic we now turn.

# Chapter 3

# The Grass Inflorescence and its Function

In most grasses vegetative growth is followed by reproductive development. In ephemeral grasses the life cycle might be completed in as little as three months whilst in some bamboos flowering may be long delayed. The switch to reproductive development in annual or monocarpic species is followed by the death of the parent plant. Even in true perennials, however, the individual reproductive shoot is monocarpic, and the continued survival of the plant depends on the further creation of vegetative tillers. Generally, seed fertility is higher in annuals than perennials, a situation readily explained since the latter need not depend entirely on the seed for propagation and spread.

The grass 'inflorescence' is a complex structure involving flowers, spikelets and panicles each of which can be regarded as a level in a hierarchy. These will be taken in turn and examined to show something of their structural contribution to grass diversity.

## The Panicle

The typical grass inflorescence is the panicle: a branching system of varying complexity which supports the spikelets (Figure 3.1). In some grasses the branching is so reduced that spikelets (in groups of 1 to 3) are directly attached to the main stem (or rachis). Such inflorescences are conventionally referred to as spikes. In some grasses such as *Alopecurus* and *Phleum* on first inspection the inflorescence is a tight spike in which branching is not apparent. Closer examination shows that these inflorescences can be understood as tightly condensed branching panicles. This is an important point, since these inflorescences are defined as panicles in floras, and must be correctly identified when using keys. *Eragrostis tef* has a range of intermediates for panicle compaction within a single species, and hybrid forms and their segregates show this to be under genetic control.

The panicle can support a uniform type of spikelet or contain more than one type. A *Tripsacum* panicle contains proximal spikelets with female florets and

Figure 3.1. Typical grass inflorescences: a) panicle of *Chrysopogon aucheri*;  b) a part of the spike of *Lolium perenne*, with the spikelets arranged edgewise to the stem and with the lower glume absent; c) the dense, compact panicle of *Phleum pratense*; d) variation in the density of panicles of *Eragrostis tef*.

distal spikelets with only male florets.  In *Zea*, a related genus, separation of the sexes has gone further with entirely male and entirely female inflorescences (the tassels and ears respectively) in the case of *Zea mays*.  A more extreme case is *Buchloë dactyloides* where male and female inflorescences occur on separate plants.  Curiously, this separation of the sexes is more pronounced in New World grasses.

## The Spikelet

One or more florets are grouped together into a spikelet (Figure 3.2) in a way broadly consistent throughout the Poaceae, but with variation in detail. The spikelet is subtended by (usually) two glumes.  Not all florets within a spikelet are functional; non-functional floret remnants occur furthest away from the

a                                                    b

Figure 3.2. Individual spikelets: a) *Poa annua*, typical pooid showing two fertile florets and a sterile remnant; b) a branch of a *Pennisetum* panicle with one fertile spikelet and, above it, several branch remnants.

glumes in pooids and nearest the glumes in panicoids. Rice is interesting from this point of view, since having one fertile floret per spikelet, and various chaffy scales, it can be viewed as either pooid or panicoid. The pooid interpretation has a single-flowered spikelet enclosed in two large glumes and subtended by two small, chaffy scales. In the panicoid interpretation, the chaffy scales are glumes subtending an elongated rachilla with two sterile lemmas and a third fertile lemma enclosing the single flower (see Chapter 4).

Around the spikelet are various appendages. In *Pennisetum* and its relatives, for example, are sterile branch remnants - an aspect of 'condensation', which is considered below. Within a floret, male and female organs may mature at different times, be absent or even atrophy. A spikelet, therefore, may have individual flowers that are hermaphrodite, male or female only, or one or more of each.

Diversity among grass spikelets is a recurrent theme in grass taxonomy and Chapter 4 presents a selection of grass spikelets illustrated in more detail.

Table 3.1. Interpretations of palea and lemma

| | Palea (two keeled) | | | Lemma (one keeled) |
|---|---|---|---|---|
| Either | Two structures, originally separate, now fused | and | either | with lemma forming a whorl of three |
| | | | or | the lemma forming a subtending bract |
| or | One structure indented by its proximity to the rachilla | and | | the lemma forming a subtending bract |

Figure 3.3. A floret of wheat made visible be removing the glume and the surrounding lemma. The two white, shiny structures at the base are the lodicules; behind them is the hairy ovary with its two feathery stigmas. Around the ovary are the three stamens with filaments not yet elongated and the whole is backed by the palea.

## The Floret (or flower)

The grass floret (Figure 3.3) consists of a pistil with two stigmas in most species, but three in the bamboos. Around this are either one or two whorls of three anthers. Beyond these are the lodicules, usually three in bamboos and two elsewhere, although species with one or no lodicules are known.

Each floret is enveloped by a pair of structures, the palea (the inner) and the lemma whose evolutionary statuses can be interpreted in more than one way. Table 3.1 sets out some of the many alternative views.

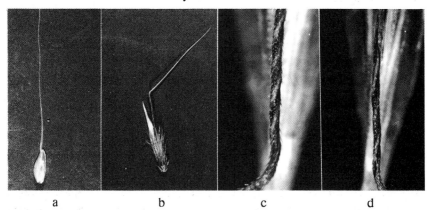

Figure 3.4. Lemmas of various species showing awns: a) the terminal awn of *Hordeum sativum*; b) the dorsal awn of *Avena fatua*; c) a closer view of b showing the tightly twisted awn structure in its dry condition; d) the same a few minutes after wetting.

The lodicules, which are thought in evolutionary terms to represent the perianth segments of grasses, normally act to force the floret open at anthesis. The palea may become fused to the caryopsis as in *Hordeum,* or may shrivel and disappear during seed development. Where florets become vestigial through the evolutionary processes of 'sterilisation' discussed below, the lemma is usually the most persistent organ and its presence is taken to indicate the possible demise of previously functional florets.

An awn may be present as a projection from the lemma (Figure 3.4). Awns can be terminal: attached to the end of the lemma as a projection of the midrib, or may be dorsal: arising from some way down the back of the midrib. Sometimes, the awn is hygroscopic and twists on being hydrated. This acts after shedding to move the dehisced grain away from the mother plant or assist in its insertion into the soil. The gluey awn of *Oplismenus* assists distribution by causing the dehisced floret to adhere to passing animals.

## Condensation - a recurrent theme

At each level in the hierarchy of floret, spikelet and panicle it is possible to detect loss of parts and compaction of the remainder when comparing different species. In some taxa, several condensations may have been superimposed, leaving in some cases hardly a trace of the original structures. Once we recognise this, it becomes evident that caution is needed in comparing distantly related grasses.

Taken altogether, the grass inflorescence is an efficient and versatile structure where the order of maturity of its spikelets and, within them, of its constituent florets offer us confusing signals about past evolutionary change and present ecological adaptation.

## Pollination and Fertilisation in Grass Sexual Reproduction

Windborne pollen is deposited on the stigma and in rye, *Secale cereale,* for example, hydration of the pollen grain from the stigma begins immediately after the 90 seconds or so required to attach the pollen grain. Thereafter germination and entry of the pollen tube and its passage to the synergid is completed for wheat within an hour and for the much longer silks of maize within about 22 hours.

The passage of the two male gametes (in reality small protoplasts referred to as gametoplasts) through the pollen tube is accompanied by a pinching off of segments of cytoplasm with plastids and mitochondria. If all the cytoplasm were removed two presumably identical nuclei would remain, but this is not apparently quite what happens. The two gametoplasts having lost much but not all of their cytoplasm proceed as follows. The one which fuses with the egg supplies only a nucleus, its residue of male cytoplasm being left on the outer surface of the egg. The other, which fuses with the central cell involves both the male nucleus and its cytoplasm. Based on the work of Mogensen (1990) double fertilisation can therefore be written for grasses as follows:

| 1 haploid male nucleus | + | 1 haploid egg nucleus and its cytoplasm | = | 1 diploid zygote nucleus in egg cytoplasm |
|---|---|---|---|---|
| 1 haploid male nucleus and its cytoplasm | + | 2 haploid polar nuclei and their cytoplasm | = | 1 triploid primary endosperm cell arising by protoplast fusion |

## Self-Incompatibility

The self-incompatibility system in grasses is apparently unique. As in some other families it is 'gametophytic' but differs in that it is a two gene system and is apparently unaffected by polyploidy. The system is illustrated in Tables 3.2 to 3.5 and is reviewed in detail by Hayman (1992).

The essentials of the grass system are that there are two loci S and Z which are unlinked and therefore segregate independently. Both S and Z consist of multi-allelic series $S_{1,2,3}...$, $Z_{1,2,3}...$. A diploid grass would therefore possess two S and two Z alleles, for example: $S_1S_2Z_1Z_2$. Style tissue is diploid and therefore possesses all four alleles whilst the pollen grain possesses one allele from each gene.

When pollen lands on the stigma, the incompatibility reaction is conditioned by whether or not the pollen grain shares alleles with that stigma and style. If it

Table 3.2. A model two gene incompatibility system showing the fate of pollen from the designated parent genotype landing on a style of genotype $S_1S_2Z_1Z_2$. The † symbol indicate pollen grain genotypes which fail.

|  | (A) | (B) | (C) | (D) |
|---|---|---|---|---|
| Pollen parent: | $S_1S_2Z_1Z_2$ | $S_1S_2Z_1Z_3$ | $S_1S_3Z_1Z_3$ | $S_3S_4Z_3Z_4$ |
| Pollen grains: | $S_1Z_1$† | $S_1Z_1$† | $S_1Z_1$† | $S_3Z_3$ |
|  | $S_1Z_2$† | $S_1Z_3$ | $S_1Z_3$ | $S_3Z_4$ |
|  | $S_2Z_1$† | $S_2Z_1$† | $S_3Z_1$ | $S_4Z_3$ |
|  | $S_2Z_2$† | $S_2Z_3$ | $S_3Z_3$ | $S_4Z_4$ |
| Result: | All alleles common: all pollen fails. | 3 alleles common: half of pollen fails. | 2 alleles common: a quarter of pollen fails. | No alleles common: no pollen fails. |

Table 3.3. Genotypes resulting from the pollinations shown in column B of Table 3.2.

| Embryo sac genotype | Functional pollen genotype | |
|---|---|---|
| | $S_1Z_3$ | $S_2Z_3$ |
| $S_1Z_1$ | $S_1S_1Z_1Z_3$ | $S_1S_2Z_1Z_3$ |
| $S_1Z_2$ | $S_1S_1Z_2Z_3$ | $S_1S_2Z_2Z_3$ |
| $S_2Z_1$ | $S_1S_2Z_1Z_3$ | $S_2S_2Z_1Z_3$ |
| $S_2Z_2$ | $S_1S_2Z_2Z_3$ | $S_2S_2Z_2Z_3$ |

Table 3.4. Genotypes resulting from the pollinations shown in column C of Table 3.2.

| Embryo sac genotype | Functional pollen genotype | | |
|---|---|---|---|
| | $S_1Z_3$ | $S_3Z_1$ | $S_3Z_3$ |
| $S_1Z_1$ | $S_1S_1Z_1Z_3$ | $S_1S_3Z_1Z_1$ | $S_1S_3Z_1Z_3$ |
| $S_1Z_2$ | $S_1S_1Z_2Z_3$ | $S_1S_3Z_1Z_2$ | $S_1S_3Z_2Z_3$ |
| $S_2Z_1$ | $S_1S_2Z_1Z_3$ | $S_2S_3Z_1Z_1$ | $S_2S_3Z_1Z_3$ |
| $S_2Z_2$ | $S_1S_2Z_2Z_3$ | $S_2S_3Z_1Z_2$ | $S_2S_3Z_2Z_3$ |

Table 3.5. Genotypes resulting from the pollinations shown in column D of Table 3.2.

| Embryo sac genotype | Functional pollen genotype | | | |
|---|---|---|---|---|
| | $S_3Z_3$ | $S_3Z_4$ | $S_4Z_3$ | $S_4Z_4$ |
| $S_1Z_1$ | $S_1S_3Z_1Z_3$ | $S_1S_3Z_1Z_4$ | $S_1S_4Z_1Z_3$ | $S_1S_4Z_1Z_4$ |
| $S_1Z_2$ | $S_1S_3Z_2Z_3$ | $S_1S_3Z_2Z_4$ | $S_1S_4Z_2Z_3$ | $S_1S_4Z_2Z_4$ |
| $S_2Z_1$ | $S_2S_3Z_1Z_3$ | $S_2S_3Z_1Z_4$ | $S_2S_4Z_1Z_3$ | $S_2S_4Z_1Z_4$ |
| $S_2Z_2$ | $S_2S_3Z_2Z_3$ | $S_2S_3Z_2Z_4$ | $S_2S_4Z_2Z_3$ | $S_2S_4Z_2Z_4$ |

shares none or one, the pollen will be compatible. If it shares both it will be incompatible. Table 3.2 indicates which pollen grains will function when assorted genotypes of pollen parent, sharing different numbers of alleles in common, are crossed to the female parent $S_1S_2Z_1Z_2$. Pollen genotypes which share both alleles in common with those present in the style, and which would therefore fail, are shown by †. For the three crosses of Table 3.2 which do produce offspring, the possible offspring genotypes are shown in Tables 3.3 to 3.5.

The following points occur:

1. Pollen having only one allele (or none) in common with the stigma will function.
2. A zygote can be homozygous at the S locus or at the Z locus but it cannot be homozygous simultaneously at both loci, e.g. $S_1S_1Z_2Z_3$ or $S_2S_3Z_1Z_1$ but not $S_2S_2Z_3Z_3$. Most zygotes are heterozygous at both loci.
3. The greater the allelic differences between two plants, the greater the likelihood that pollen will function. Within a population this mechanism greatly increases the probability of successful cross pollination, since the number of cross-compatible genotypes is related to the product of the number of alleles for each gene. Most estimates have identified some tens of alleles for each gene, resulting in hundreds of cross-compatible combinations.
4. Grass pollen is often produced in vast quantities and is in that sense 'expendable'. The ovary produces one ovule only and is thus a valued resource. It is worth commenting that on the basis of incompatibility reactions no ovule is wasted though, of course, for other reasons such as lack of physiological support or some kind of damage it may fail.

SZ incompatibility is unusual in that the incompatibility reaction is retained in polyploids. Any SZ allelic combination present in the pollen grain, which is also present in the style, gives an incompatible reaction (Hayman, 1992). Many problems about the grass incompatibility system remain unanswered. They include the following. We do not know if the SZ system is unique to grasses or whether all self-compatible grasses have become so by degeneration of SZ. It is not clear why polyploidy leaves the system intact (as compared with gametophytic systems elsewhere) nor has any significant progress been made in a molecular understanding of the pollen-stigma interaction.

# Chapter 4

# Diversity in the Grass Spikelet

In the previous chapter the spikelet was treated as one component of the inflorescence. It is however a structure that exists in many forms and is important for grass taxonomy. A range of types is examined here to indicate something of spikelet diversity although the reader should recognise it represents a small sample only.

By a spikelet is normally meant a pair of glumes at the base of a rachilla on which are borne one or more florets. This theme is the basis of many variations. Glumes can be fewer or more than two, florets can be hermaphrodite, male or female, or vestigial perhaps represented by no more than a lemma. All manner of additional detail can be present such as hairs, bristles or markings and various kinds of awn. Spikelets may have many florets or the florets themselves may be in some way unusual or even grotesque when for example in the bamboo *Ochlandra*, anther number per floret rises above a hundred. The lower glume of *Thyridolepis* has bristles and a curious hyaline (translucent) patch. Lodicules are absent from *Rhizocephalus* for example. In *Lolium* the spikelet is set edgeways on to the rachis. *Zea* has male and female spikelets in different inflorescences on the same plant and *Buchloë* can be monoecious as is *Zea* or dioecious with male and female spikelets on separate plants.

Despite such diversity, with practice the spikelet is normally a recognisable unit. An obvious exception is in *Zea* where the congested arrangement of spikelets on the female inflorescence is far from straightforward to resolve. A curious feature of *Zea* is that various mutant alternatives affect only the female spikelet although other mutants are known that affect the distribution of male and female spikelets on the various inflorescences. In seeking to resolve details of the maize ear it is instructive to examine its relatives, notably *Zea diploperennis, Z. mexicana* and various species of *Tripsacum*.

## Spikelet Examination

It is easier to examine spikelet detail in the green stages rather than when ripening has begun since the tissues then harden. Examination is considerably simplified with access to a binocular dissecting microscope, a sharp scalpel, fine forceps and a pair of mounted needles, these last being especially useful. (Periodically it will be necessary to sharpen them.) It is sometimes recommended to use an eyeglass or a handlens but neither is as convenient as a dissecting microscope, which in any case is, nowadays, a commonplace piece of standard laboratory equipment. Especially with very delicate spikelets it is better to use reflected than transmitted light since the tissues are then less readily dehydrated.

The illustrated examples set out in this chapter follow a selected taxonomic arrangement intended as a preliminary to Chapter 5.

## A Range of Spikelets Compared

To facilitate comparison and cross reference, in the following pages the lower glume is normally shown pointing left. Not every aspect is labelled, attention being concentrated upon features selected for comparison. The following symbols are used:

| | | | |
|---|---|---|---|
| A | anther | MS | median spikelet |
| At | attachment point of rachis to spikelets | O | ovary |
| | | P | palea |
| C | caryopsis | PS | pedicellate spikelet |
| F | floret | R | rachilla |
| FL | flag leaf | S | spikelet |
| G | glume | Sc | sterile spikelet |
| H | hair | SS | sessile spikelet |
| I | inflorescence | St | stigma/style |
| IB | inflorescence branch | UG | upper glume |
| L | lemma | UL | upper lemma |
| LG | lower glume | ♀ | female |
| LL | lower lemma | ☿ | hermaphrodite |
| Lo | lodicule | ♂ | male |
| LS | lateral spikelet | | |

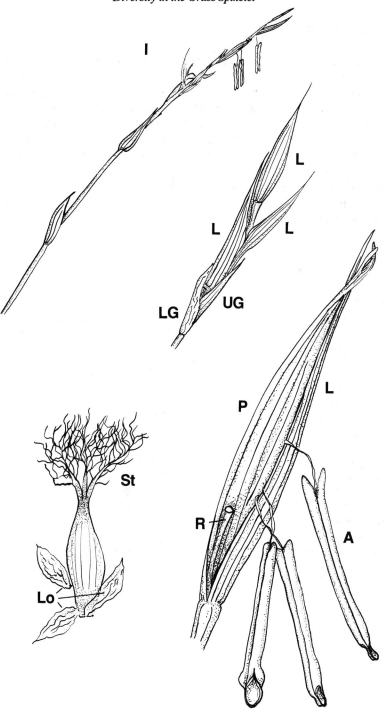

Figure 4.1. The inflorescence of *Arundinaria gigantea.*

| **1. Bamboo** | subfamily | Bambusoideae |
| | tribe | Bambuseae |
| | subtribe | Arundinariinae |
| | genus and species | *Arundinaria gigantea* |

*Arundinaria* is a warm temperate genus of bamboo occurring naturally in China. As long lived perennials they are interesting to horticulturists since various off-types or chimaeras with yellow leaves and/or stems provide ornamentals sufficiently hardy for northern Europe. See for example Chao (1989).

The species shown in Figure 4.1 illustrates several interesting features. The inflorescence (left) consists of a single spikelet. It is open to speculation whether this is primitive or is derived by reduction from some more complex ancestral arrangement. There are two glumes and above them three separate florets. Unlike the grasses that follow, the stigma is *three* branched and there are three lodicules: each, arguably, a primitive condition.

Flowering in some bamboos is preceded by many years of vegetative growth and with distinctive and regular intervals characteristic of a particular species. For a detailed review see Janzen (1976). It is known however that individual plants can flower spasmodically, a feature utilised in current work to breed bamboos artificially.

| **2. *Ehrharta*** | subfamily | Bambusoideae |
| | tribe | Ehrharteae |
| | genus and species | *Ehrharta erecta* |

*Ehrharta* is a genus occurring naturally in the southern hemisphere but can occur as an occasional in the north temperate flora. See Stace (1991).

In the example shown (Figure 4.2) the inflorescence is an open panicle with each spikelet on a long rachis. In the centre a single spikelet is displayed with the following interesting features. Above the glumes are empty lemmas ($L_1$, $L_2$) interpreted as vestigial florets. F indicates the single, functional floret.

If the lower and upper glumes were diminished almost to extinction and $L_1$ and $L_2$ appreciably reduced, some affinity to rice can be conjectured (compare with the next illustration). Both *Ehrharta* and rice are 'bambusoid' grasses, each with six anthers per floret, but with only two lodicules. (One might then say 'lodicules reduced to two' implying an evolutionary sequence.)

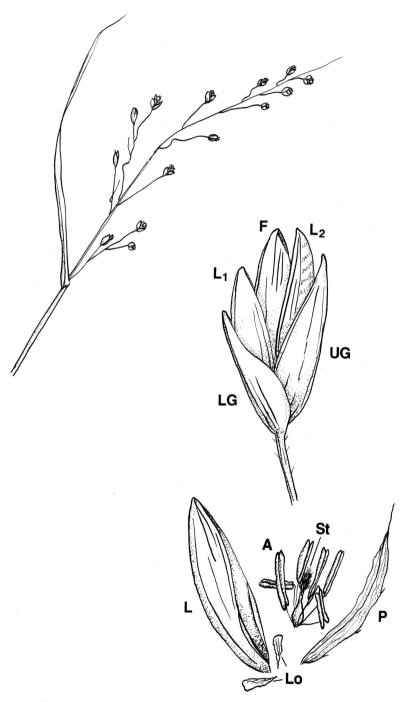

Figure 4.2. The inflorescence of *Ehrharta erecta*.

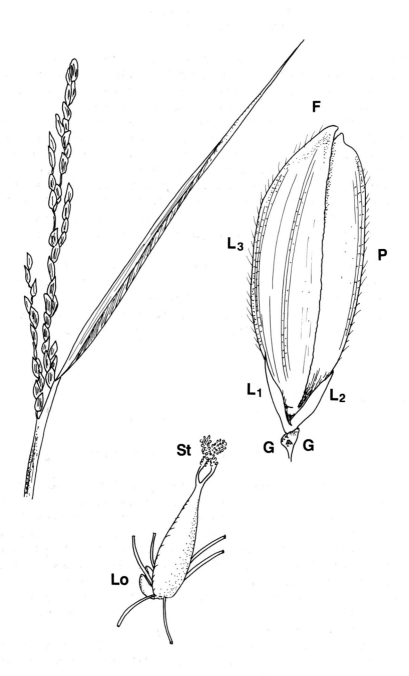

Figure 4.3. The inflorescence of *Oryza sativa*.

**3. Rice**  subfamily    Bambusoideae
        tribe        Oryzeae
        genus and species    *Oryza sativa*

Most genera in the Oryzeae inhabit aquatic or at least moist environments. The genus *Oryza* was separately domesticated in Asia and West Africa. In the former *O. nivara* is thought to have given rise to *O. sativa* and in the latter the wild *O. barthii* is the presumed immediate ancestor of *O glaberrima*.

The following features are illustrated (Figure 4.3). A panicle is shown with the typically clustered arrangement of spikelets. Mention has already been made of a possible affinity with *Ehrharta*. Can, however, the rice spikelet be viewed in another way? Suppose that what are labelled as glumes here are regarded instead as unnamed chaffy scales. We could then regard the lemmas lower and upper glumes subtending a single flower. Suppose now that above these glumes there had been, much earlier in evolution, several florets of which all but the one immediately above the glumes has disappeared, i.e progressive loss of function *down* the spikelet.

The point of interest is that we could, theoretically devise a rice spikelet either from something like *Ehrharta* or from some other ancestor in the way just outlined. In this connection, see *Poa* and *Panicum*.

All *Oryza* species are hermaphrodite, but in the related genus *Zizania* (American Rice) the panicle has male spikelets towards the base and female spikelets towards the apex.

## 4. Common Reed

            subfamily    Arundinoideae
            tribe        Arundineae
            genus and species    *Phragmites australis*

Among the more familiar genera in this subfamily are *Phragmites* (reed), *Arundo* and *Cortaderia* – all large grasses with large plumed panicles. *Thysanolaena* from tropical Asia has a similar appearance. Less familiar is *Aristida* (p. 34).

The tribe Arundineae is illustrated with a spikelet of *P. australis* separated into its constituent florets (Figure 4.4). Above the glumes, the lowest floret is male and above this all others are hermaphrodite. Each consists of a larger lemma and smaller palea the latter with its edges reflexed away from the lemma. The awns are more conspicuous on the lemmas furthest from the glumes. Each floret rachilla is invested with fine hairs. Curiously, in this plant seed-setting is rare and the plant reproduces mostly vegetatively.

*Phragmites* is used for making screens from its cane-like stems but lacks the durability of bamboo. It is sometimes recommended in marshy areas for moderating the effects of pollution.

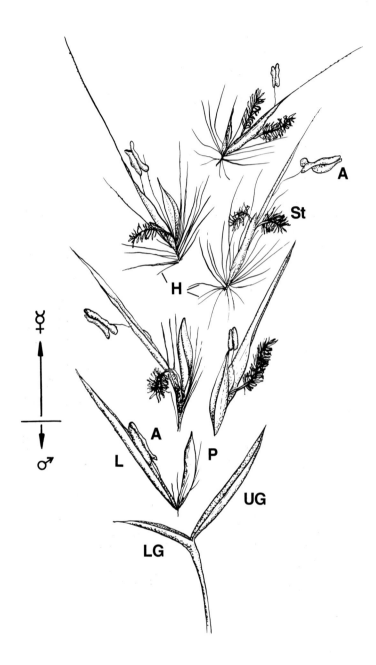

Figure 4.4. The inflorescence of *Phragmites australis.*

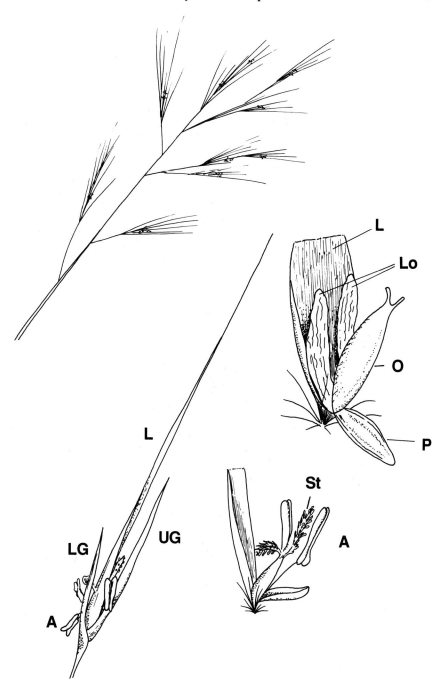

Figure 4.5. The inflorescence of *Aristida funiculata*.

**5. *Aristida***          subfamily          Arundinoideae
                          tribe              Aristideae
                          genus and species  *Aristida funiculata*

Three genera, *Aristida*, *Sartidia* and *Stipagrostis* comprise the Aristideae, of which the first is the largest genus, estimated to have around 300 species.

The three genera can be definitively separated on leaf anatomy, *Aristida* having specialised Kranz anatomy, *Sartidia* being non-Kranz and *Stipagrostis* conventional Kranz. At a practical level the genera are separated by the awn and glume characters. Only *Stipagrostis* has plumose awns whilst *Sartidia* has three and *Aristida* has one vein in the glume.

Within *Aristida* the awn varies considerably and can be used to divide the genus into sections. The example shown here (Figure 4.5) possesses a simple, though obviously prolonged awn. *Aristida* contains both annual and perennial species, some of which provide useful grazing in warm semi-arid to arid regions.


## 6. Annual Meadow Grass

                          subfamily          Pooideae
                          tribe              Poeae
                          genus and species  *Poa annua*

*Poa* is one of the largest grass genera with about 500 species distributed throughout the cool temperate regions. It is a genus from which, probably, many other genera have been derived.

*Poa annua* is highly cosmopolitan, extending into the warmer regions. It occurs as a common weed in temperate lawns and grows on a wide variety of soil types. Flowering and seeding plants can be found throughout most of the year. This, together with its soft tissues and relatively simple spikelet structure make it an ideal subject with which to introduce grass reproductive structure.

The central diagram (Figure 4.6) shows typical spikelets, although the number may vary from two (rarely) to eight or more. Close examination of the spikelet normally shows, at the top of the rachilla, a rudimentary floret represented by little more than a diminished lemma. Compare this with the structure of *Oryza* and *Panicum*.


## 7. Barley

                          subfamily          Pooideae
                          tribe              Triticeae
                          genus and species  *Hordeum sativum*

The Triticeae is a tribe of major economic importance since it includes wheat, barley and rye together with a group of undomesticated genera that provide useful genes in cereal breeding programmes. Taxonomists have adopted various

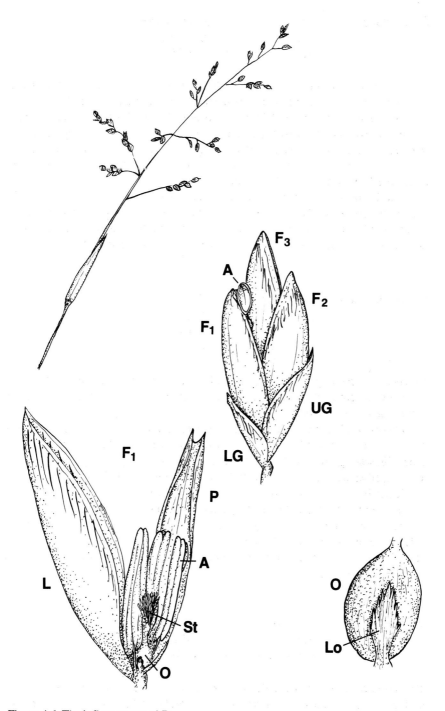

Figure 4.6. The inflorescence of *Poa annua*.

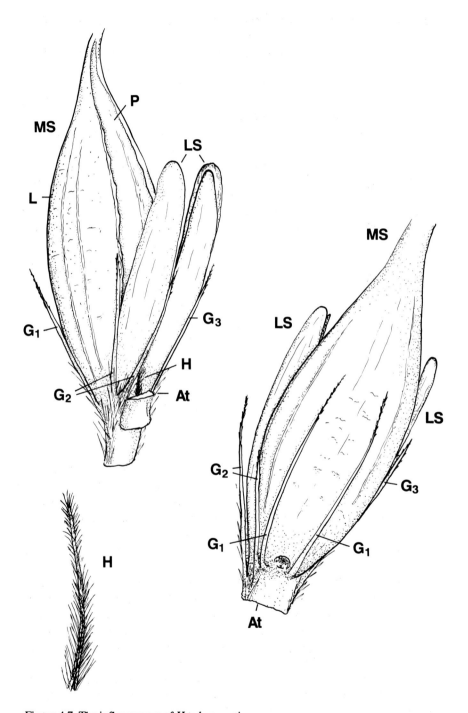

Figure 4.7. The inflorescence of *Hordeum sativum*.

approaches to the Triticeae and a part of their difficulty is the readiness of different species to hybridise across generic boundaries.

*Hordeum sativum* is illustrated here in relation to grain row number (Figure 4.7). The spikelet clusters are taken from opposite sides of a barley spike. In each case there is one large functional spikelet flanked by two abortive spikelets. The result is a 'two rowed' barley. If all three spikelets functioned (on either side of the spike) the barley is 'six rowed'.

An important point to grasp when comparing barley with wheat is that three closely associated grains of wheat are the product of a single spikelet whereas (in six rowed barley) three closely associated grains arise in separate spikelets.

A point of interest about the functional median spikelets (MS) opposite is their pairs of glumes labelled $G_1$. These are of equal status and not conveniently separable into upper and lower. The glumes stand side-by-side in front of the lemma. For the non-functional lateral spikelets, $G_2$ indicates the two subtending glumes of one and $G_3$ the only visible one of the two subtending the other lateral spikelet. The label At indicates the point of attachment of the rachis. The branched hair (H) is interpreted as an extension of the rachilla (compare this with *Pennisetum* below).

The lemmas are extended into long awns (not drawn) that give barley its characteristic bearded appearance. Several mutants affecting the shape of the awns are known (see Chapter 8).

## 8. Kallar Grass

| | |
|---|---|
| subfamily | Chloridoideae |
| tribe | Eragrostideae |
| subtribe | Eleusininae |
| genus and species | *Leptochloa fusca* |

The subfamily Chlorideae is uniformly $C_4$ with Kranz anatomy (see Chapter 6), typically adapted to warm dry regions and containing some of the most drought tolerant grasses known. The microhairs of chloridoid grasses such as *Leptochloa* can function as salt glands so that when they are grown in salted soil they can secrete salt on their leaf surfaces. By growing these species on soils damaged by poor irrigation practice, the soil can be rehabilitated. Removing the salt-laden foliage removes salt from the soil.

The panicle illustrated (Figure 4.8) is relatively open, with branches arranged approximately in whorls. IB is part of an inflorescence branch showing the sinuous rachis with ridges of bristles running lengthwise and clusters of spikelets. The single spikelet (lower centre) shows that the distal or terminal floret (Sc) is sterile or vestigial. Although reminiscent of *Poa* in this respect, *Leptochloa* is $C_4$ and incorporates many other differences.

Lower left a single floret at seed maturity has been opened to show the lemma and the reflexed palea backing on to the rachilla which would support the next floret. Lower right the caryopsis still shows anther and stigma remnants.

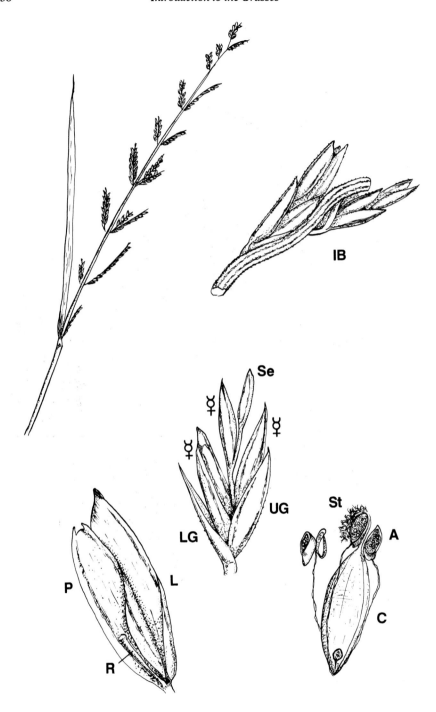

Figure 4.8. The inflorescence of *Leptochloa fusca*.

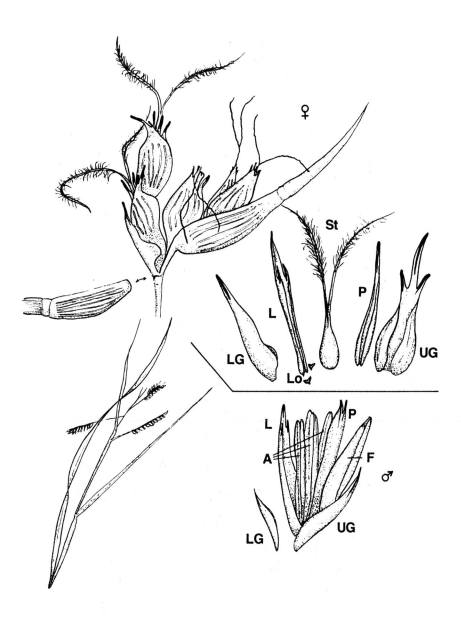

Figure 4.9. The inflorescence of *Buchloë dactyloides*.

## 9. Buffalo Grass

| | |
|---|---|
| subfamily | Chloridoideae |
| tribe | Cynodonteae |
| subtribe | Boutelouinae |
| genus and species | *Buchloë dactyloides* |

The subtribe Boutelouinae includes several genera such as *Buchlomimus, Cyclostachya* and *Pringlechloa* which all have some degree of separation of the sexes. In *Buchloë dactyloides*, however, any batch of seeds will produce some plants which are exclusively male, some female and a few which bear both male and female (separate) inflorescences. Variants also exist for anther colour which can be cream, yellow or apricot.

At first sight, the inflorescences of male and female plants are so different that they might appear to belong to different species, but closer examination reveals some similarities (Figure 4.9). The line in the diagrams separates male and female structures. The female inflorescence shows two characteristic clusters of spikelets. In both sexes, the upper glume is larger than the lower, and similar green markings are found in glumes, lemmas and paleas. The lemma of each is similarly subdivided. Note, however, that the female spikelet is one-flowered whilst that of the male is two-flowered. (L - P encompasses the open flower and F the closed flower, lower right.)

## 10. A Pearl Millet Derivative

| | |
|---|---|
| subfamily | Panicoideae |
| tribe | Paniceae |
| subtribe | Cenchrinae |
| genus and species | *Pennisetum ((glaucum × squamulatum)* |

The subtribe Cenchrinae includes *Anthephora, Cenchrus* and *Pennisetum*, all having important pasture species in the tropics. Additionally *Pennisetum glaucum* provides pearl or bulrush millet, an important cereal.

*Pennisetum glaucum* was hybridised to a wild species, *P. squamulatum*, and a number of segregating offspring obtained, of which one is shown opposite.

The inflorescence shown here is 'hairy' (Figure 4.10). The hairs (similar in appearance to those of *Hordeum*) are interpreted here as sterile branch remnants of a once more branching panicle. These cluster round a short productive branch bearing clusters of spikelets(S). One is currently open with its stigma exposed, demonstrating functional protogyny.

Lower centre, a spikelet has been opened to show the following features: above the lower glume is a structure L, all that can be detected of the lower floret. Above the upper glume (UG) is the upper lemma L with its palea enclosing three anthers (A). This floret lacks female organs.

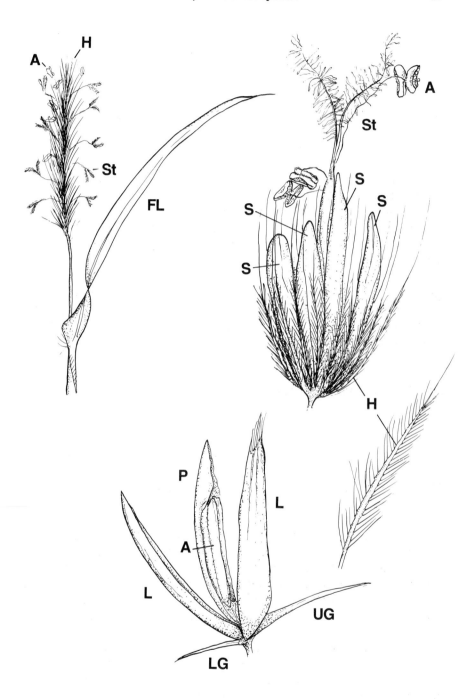

Figure 4.10. The inflorescence of *Pennisetum (glaucum × squamulatum)*.

## 11. Guinea Grass

| | |
|---|---|
| subfamily | Panicoideae |
| tribe | Paniceae |
| subtribe | Setariinae |
| genus and species | *Panicum maximum* |

The Panicoideae embraces a most diverse group of grasses. Although found in all latitudes it is primarily tropical and subtropical. The tribe Paniceae is divided into four subtribes of which the Setariinae includes *Panicum, Paspalum* and *Brachiaria* – all important pasture grasses. *Echinochloa* and *Setaria* provide minor cereals and *Axonopus* is a lawn grass in the moist tropics. The genus *Panicum* is one of the largest in the entire grass family with nearly five hundred species including the cereal *Panicum mileaceum.* Species with $C_3$, various types of $C_4$ and intermediate photosythetic mechanisms all occur in the genus. It is probably realistic to regard *Panicum* as the origin from which many derivative genera have sprung. The grass illustrated here  (Figure 4.11) is an apomict and a species of major consequence in the tropics. Guinea grass is a robust perennial found in unimproved pastures and along roadsides and upon which for example the cows and goats of poorer people heavily depend.

To the upper left is shown an open multibranched panicle.  Spikelets are clustered along the branches (not all illustrated here). A spikelet at late anthesis is shown with relatively compact anthers (cf. those of *Pennisetum* for example). Note the fairly conspicuous longitudinal ridges and the small though conspicuous lower glume. Below, turned through 90°, the glumes, lemmas and paleas are set out in order. Working clockwise - small lower glume, lower lemma, upper palea, upper lemma, upper glume. The commonly accepted interpretation is that the lower lemma represents the vestigial  lower floret. The upper palea and upper lemma enclose the functioning  upper floret of which the sex organs are illustrated. It will now be apparent that, while in *Poa* the vestigial lemmas occur at the top of the spikelet, they occur at the base, above the glumes, in *Panicum*. Loss of floral function (sterilisation) is thus conjectured to be from the top downward in *Poa* and from the bottom upward in *Panicum*. Even if one rejects the evolutionary implication, it is helpful to recognise these typically 'pooid' and 'panicoid' spikelet arrangements. Refer back also to the discussions of *Oryza* and *Ehrharta.*

Note that the lower lemma and the upper glume effectively enclose the  mature grain and that the entire structure is shed as a unit.

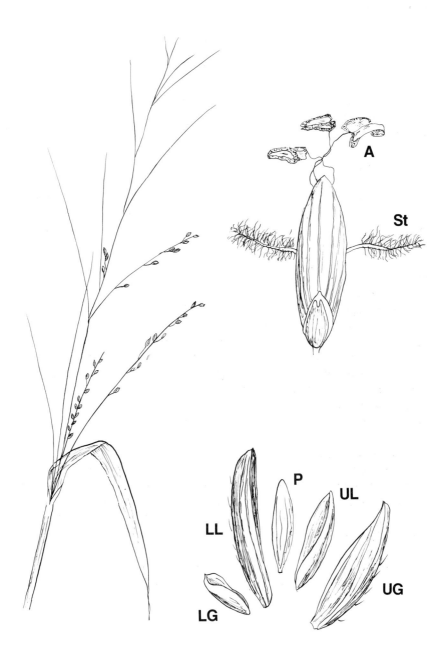

Figure 4.11. The inflorescence of *Panicum maximum*.

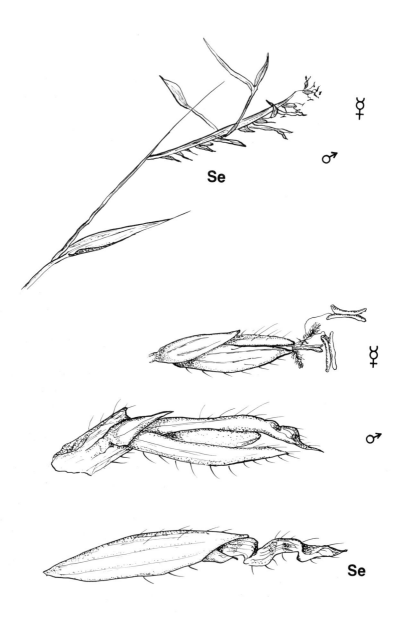

Figure 4.12. The inflorescence of *Brachiaria decumbens*.

## 12. *Brachiaria*

| | |
|---|---|
| subfamily | Panicoideae |
| tribe | Paniceae |
| subtribe | Setariinae |
| genus and species | *Brachiaria decumbens* |

*Brachiaria* is a genus closely related to *Panicum*. The material shown here illustrates prolifery (or vivipary) where a spikelet is converted to a small plantlet.

The uppermost diagram (Figure 4.12) shows spikelets from different parts of the inflorescence that are hermaphrodite, male and sterile respectively. The three lower diagrams show spikelets in greater detail. The lowest one has been transformed to a small plantlet, potentially a means of vegetative reproduction.

## 13. Perennial Teosinte

| | |
|---|---|
| subfamily | Panicoideae |
| tribe | Andropogoneae |
| subtribe | Tripsacinae |
| genus and species | *Zea diploperennis* |

A feature of the Andropogoneae is the presence of paired spikelets - one sessile and one pedicellate, that is on a short stalk. It is a theme capable of considerable variation and the tribe includes many important grasses such as *Saccharum* (sugar cane) *Sorghum* and *Zea* (maize). The subtribe Tripsacinae includes *Zea mays* and wild species of *Zea* and *Tripsacum* .

The maize plant is extraordinary and is known only in cultivation. How it might have derived from wild grasses provides a story of absorbing botanical detective work that is not yet complete. It is important to recognise that the female ear borne laterally and the male tassel held terminally are a departure from wild grasses. The example illustrated here is *Zea diploperennis* perhaps the crop plant's closest wild relative though recognisably different from it.

Features of interest in the diagrams include the inflorescence showing the very long styles (Figure 4.13). The spikelets are paired with the sessile spikelet being bulbous and female while beside it is the spear-shaped male pedicellate spikelet. In Figure 4.14 the sessile spikelet is shown opened out, except for the upper glume which has been omitted. This has a typical panicoid arrangement. The lower glume subtends only a lemma. All the remaining structures: palea, caryopsis, two lodicules and the upper lemma comprise the functional floret which was subtended by the upper glume.

Note: in *Zea mays* separation of the sexes has gone further. The ear consists only of paired female spikelets, both sessile. The tassel, in contrast, contains only male spikelets, but with the expected sessile/pedicellate pairing. In *Sorghum* the sessile spikelet is hermaphrodite and the pedicellate spikelet non-functional.

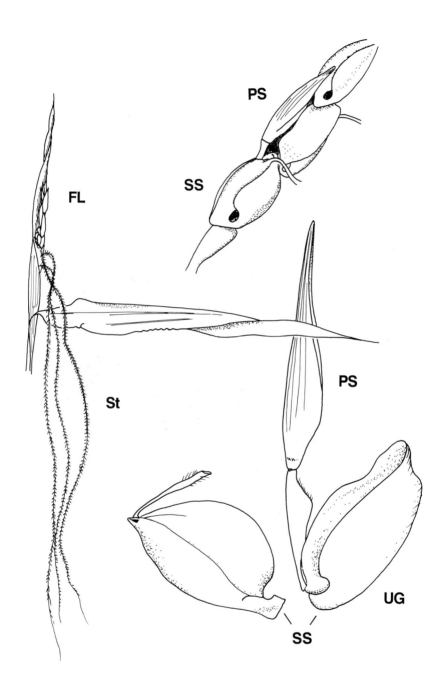

Figure 4.13. The inflorescence of *Zea diploperennis*.

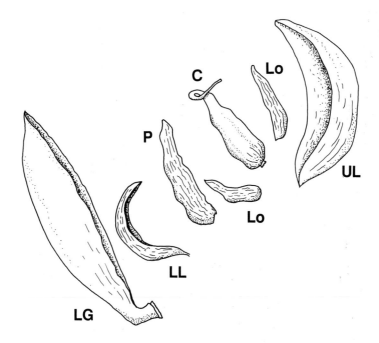

Figure 4.14. A dissected, female spikelet of *Zea diploperennis*.

# Chapter 5

# Taxonomy

Two recent and important references to grass taxonomy are those of Clayton and Renvoize (1986) and Watson and Dallwitz (1988, 1992), which have interesting differences in approach. The first is a traditional style text, illustrated with helpful interpretive diagrams which explain the authors' views of relationships among grasses. The second has been developed from a computer database of information on all grass genera, derived from a wide range of sources and continually updated. This allows any user to compare and classify entries, or to identify an unknown specimen. The latest version of this database, describing 785 grass genera by 496 characters has been published in book form (Watson and Dallwitz, 1992). Neither system is exclusive of the other and the most practicable approach is to use them both, as we have done in preparing this book. In this chapter we give some brief indications of how the two systems differ in their assessment of the Poaceae.

One of the major uses of taxonomy by botanists at large is the reliable identification of species. Such identification depends on the ready availability of regional floras. Ideally these would be based on continuous revisions utilising shifts in our knowledge of the relevant area coupled with new taxonomic insights. In reality, the situation is one of scarce resources spread too thinly and many regional floras are old and out of date, even though representing in many cases the immense commitment and energy of earlier botanists. A collaborative programme of training whereby young scientists work at the major herbaria, using the revisions of their own country's flora as a basis, though obviously desirable, is poorly funded at present. Details of regional floras can be obtained from Frodin (1984).

Watson and Dallwitz's (1992) database in its computer-accessible form, although restricted to generic descriptions, presents an interesting alternative. Firstly, searches through the data can be restricted to sets of genera known to exist in a locality. Secondly, the character descriptions can be matched to an unknown specimen in any order the user chooses. This is much more flexible than the conventional structure of a written key. Finally, the program itself will suggest which are the 'best' characters to use in discriminating between the genera.

# Major Taxonomic Divisions of the Poaceae

Modern assessments of grasses recognise five major subfamilies, each of which can be divided into tribes, subtribes, genera and eventually species. The descriptions below indicate the major characteristics which distinguish one subfamily from the rest. Some of the terms used may be unfamiliar and for these the reader is referred to the glossary. More detailed descriptions are given by Watson (1990) and Clayton and Renvoize (1992).

## Bambusoideae: the bamboos

This is probably the most primitive subfamily in terms of flower structure, although it is unlikely that it now contains the origin of grasses, since in evolutionary terms even this group has moved on. None the less, it is believed to provide valuable clues to grass origins. This is a group in which fusoid and arm cells are commonly observed in leaf sections. The inflorescence can be either complex or very simple panicles and the leaves have membranous ligules. Many species have trimerous flowers, compared with the more common distichous structure (see Figures 4.1 - 4.3). The name of the subfamily is obviously derived from the woody culm (bamboos) which many, but not all members of the group possess. Two genera containing crop plants, both rices, *Oryza* and *Zizania*, occur in this large assemblage.

According to Clayton and Renvoize (1986) the subfamily is subdivided into thirteen tribes of which the largest (Bambuseae) is again divided into three subtribes. Watson's (1990) arrangement is not dissimilar and it is noteworthy that both systems accept a series of largely similar tribes.

## Arundinoideae

Although some species with $C_4$ photosynthesis do occur in this subfamily, they are typically $C_3$ with non-Kranz leaf anatomy. Plants are herbs or large reeds, the ligule is typically ciliate and the lemmas bilobed and awned from the sinus.

No cereals occur here but familiar representatives are pampas grass (*Cortaderia*) and reed (*Phragmites*: Figure 4.4).

The term 'relict' is applied to this subfamily and its prominence in the southern hemisphere has been explained as a refuge or retreat habitat for a group unable to compete elsewhere. If this is so the large and successful genus *Aristida* (Figure 4.5) with about 300 species and $C_4$ photosynthesis provides a marked contrast. Renvoize and Clayton (1992) point out that many features found elsewhere in herbage grasses occur in the Arundinoideae and this seems to support their view that it is ancestral. Nonetheless its tribe, Micraireae is unusual with a moss-like habit and spiral phyllotaxy.

The treatments of Arundinoideae by Clayton and Renvoize and Watson are compared in detail later.

## Pooideae

A large group of grasses with membranous ligules and mostly temperate in distribution. They all possess the non-Kranz leaf anatomy typical of species with $C_3$ photosynthesis. The spikelets are relatively unspecialised, with the fertile florets concentrated at the base and sterile florets above (Figures 4.6 and 4.7). It has been suggested, however, that these obvious features are of less consequence in defining the subfamily than are internal changes. Clayton and Renvoize (1986) for example draw attention to modifications of the endosperm (especially in the tribes Aveneae and Bromeae) and to the larger chromosomes found in this subfamily.

Several crop plants occur here including oats (*Avena*), barley (*Hordeum*, Figure 4.7), rye (*Secale*) and wheat (*Triticum*) and the forage grasses fescue (*Festuca*) and ryegrass (*Lolium*).

Clayton and Renvoize recognise ten tribes but Watson uses fewer larger groupings. Each system identifies the Triticeae (a name common to both) as problematic due in part to the ease with which hybridisation has occurred among its closely related yet individually distinctive genera. Both *Hordeum* and *Triticum* belong here and under appropriate conditions even such distinct genera as these can be induced to hybridise.

## Chloridoideae

A subfamily whose species are frequent in the tropics and which show two variants of $C_4$ photosynthesis (NAD-ME and PEP-CK: see Chapter 6). Typically, chloridoid grasses have unilateral racemes and compressed, many-flowered spikelets. A small minority belong to the so-called 'resurrection' grasses.

Cereals include millet (*Eleusine*), and t'ef (*Eragrostis tef*). There are also important forages such as the Mitchell grasses (*Astrebla* spp.), Rhodes grass (*Chloris gayana*) and Bermuda grass (*Cynodon dactylon*). Of interest too is Kallar grass (*Leptochloa fusca*, Figure 4.8), which is able to remove salt from soils degraded for example by poor irrigation practice.

Clayton and Renvoize recognise five tribes of which two are subdivided into subtribes. Although there are some differences of treatment by Watson the limits of this subfamily (what does and does not belong here) are generally agreed.

## Panicoideae

The spikelets typically show an opposite structure to that of Pooideae, with a sterile floret at the base and a fertile one above. The spikelets often fall entire. Both $C_3$ and all types of $C_4$ photosynthesis occur here, although the important andropogonoid group is exclusively $C_4$ with NADP-ME metabolism.

The subfamily is largely though not exclusively tropical and although the basic chromosome number, n = 10, is common, there are departures from this.

Cereals occurring here include the millets (*Echinochloa crus-galli, Panicum miliaceum, Setaria italica*), sorghum (*Sorghum bicolor*) and maize (*Zea mays*). Forages include Surinam grass (*Brachiaria decumbens*, Figure 4.12), Pangola grass (*Digitaria eriantha*), Buffel grass (*Cenchrus ciliaris*) and Bahia grass (*Paspalum notatum*).

Among other noteworthy grasses are sugar cane (*Saccharum officinarum*) where the solid stems store large quantities of commercially extractable sucrose and Vetiver grass (*Vetiveria zizanioides*) which is important both as a source of aromatic oil and as a goat-resistant barrier against soil erosion.

As will be evident from the discussion below of Arundinoideae the two taxonomic systems do not agree exactly about the limits of either the Pooideae or the Panicoideae. Aside from this each system recognises major groupings within the Panicoideae around the panicoid and andropogonoid grasses. Small subgroups such as *Neurachne* and its associates are jointly recognised as distinct. (The Neurachninae of the one and the Neurachneae of the other both include the same three genera.)

An interesting difference emerges over an economically important group - maize and its associates. The same genera placed in three subtribes by Clayton and Renvoize are pooled into one group by Watson.

**Centothecoideae: a note** Clayton and Renvoize (1986) but not Watson follow Söderstrom (1981) in accepting this small subfamily of ten genera and about 30 species. Its likely affinities are with bamboos and arundinoids. No cereal genera are included.

## Two Classifications Compared

The two systems of grass classification, of Clayton and Renvoize (1986) and (1992) (summarised) and of Watson (summarised) (1990) are widely used. Differences of presentation have been mentioned already but they also differ in the taxonomic conclusions that they reach. The Arundinoideae, the smallest subfamily common to both systems, provides a convenient example to illustrate this, summarised in Table 5.1.

The two systems broadly agree on what falls within or outside this subfamily. Note too that both systems agree on the genera comprising the tribes that Clayton and Renvoize place in the Panicoideae rather than in the Arundinoideae. The largest tribe recognised by Clayton and Renvoize, the Arundineae is split into three by Watson, but again substantially the same genera are involved.

The Aristideae includes the same genera in both systems, as does the Micraireae of Clayton and Renvoize (= the Micrairieae of Watson).

Finally it is worth noting that in a revision of their system Clayton and Renvoize (1992) have (a) added *Cyperochloa* not as a tribe but as a genus within

Arundineae, (b) abandoned the tribe Thysanolaeneae and placed its single genus in the tribe Arundineae.

**Harmonisation?** Ought we to try and harmonise the two systems or even merge them into one? Surely it would be more 'convenient'? In fact, such uniformity would be misleading because taxonomic understanding continues to develop. Genera continue to be split off or pooled with other genera, not out of whim, but because slowly, our appreciation of what is truly distinct alters and, we believe, improves. For a more detailed discussion of the present state of grass taxonomy see Watson (1990).

Table 5.1. A comparison of the tribes contained within the subfamily Arundinoideae, using the classifications of Clayton and Renvoize (1986) and Watson (1990). Numbers of genera in brackets.

| Watson | Clayton and Renvoize |
|---|---|
| Stipeae (14) Nardeae (1) Lygeae (1) | tribes of subfamily Pooideae |
| Steyermarkochloeae (2) Eriachneae (2) | tribes of subfamily Panicoideae |
| Arundineae (2) Danthonieae (44) Spartochloeae (1) | Arundineae (40) |
| Cyperochloeae (1) | - |
| Micrairieae (1) | Micraireae (1) |
| Aristideae (3) | Aristideae (3) |
| - | Thysanolaeneae (1) |

# Tribes, Genera and Species

## Tribes

Of what significance is the tribe for the grass taxonomist and for other workers involved with the family? Chapman (1990) examined the frequency of 'wide' crossing among the grasses and it is evident that most inter-generic crosses occur within a tribe. The minority of authentic inter-tribal crosses which are known are rare, difficult to achieve and almost invariably attended by genetic malfunction. Tribal boundaries, therefore, do seem to have some biological meaning which can be used by other workers in addition to taxonomists.

# Genera

If respectable taxonomists cannot agree on the limits of a genus of what signifi-cance is it? In a curious way the genus is quite remarkable and it was for Linnaeus, for example, probably his most important unit. There is a 'solidity' about the genus which many biologists recognise even though they might have difficulty with tribal affinities or the identity of a particular species. When iden-tifying grasses (or indeed other plants) the genus often springs to mind, the real effort being required to identify the species.

Does this beg the question, then, as to why taxonomists cannot agree on the limits of a genus? The answer is that in trying to define the limits of a genus taxonomists are simply aware of more species (than are the majority of biologists) that may or may not belong. Many and perhaps most disagreements are about hard cases.

An interesting case is that of *Festuca* (450 spp.) and *Lolium* (8 spp.). The two genera are readily distinguished morphologically. However, *F. pratensis*, which will not hybridise with some other fescues, will hybridise with *Lolium perenne* and the hybrid is recognised in nature as × *Festulolium*. A parallel situa-tion occurs with *F. arundinacea* and *L. perenne*. For these species of *Festuca* and *Lolium*, as regards their relationships, crossability points one way and mor-phology the other. The matter can be understood by recognising that the larger genus *Festuca* has affinities in several directions with contrasted genera. *Lolium*, although distinct, none the less displays a genetic affinity through *F. arundi-nacea* and *F. pratensis* with part of *Festuca* and this may indicate something of the origins of *Lolium* from within *Festuca*.

However differences may strike the student, it is probably true to say now that, after more than a century of intensive study, the main themes in grass tax-onomy have emerged and that things are beginning to settle down.

The problem for biologists at large is that changes to the limits of a genus involve consequential changes in the names of the affected species. Name changes may be the taxonomists' expression of second thoughts, but they are fre-quently seen as an inconvenience or worse by non-taxonomists. An example concerns the genus *Stipagrostis* sometimes subsumed under *Aristida*. Should *Stipagrostis* be separated or not? As new information has accumulated two characters tend to occur together. These are plumose awns and Kranz leaf anatomy ($C_4$, NAD-ME). If such species (formerly in *Aristida*) are removed to *Stipagrostis* the remaining *Aristida* species have non-plumose awns and a highly specialised $C_4$ leaf structure not known elsewhere. Having drawn a distinction here it becomes evident that particular characters tend to be associated with ei-ther *Aristida* or *Stipagrostis*. On balance taxonomists are inclined to accept that two genera rather than one genus fairly represents the situation but clearly in the end it is a matter of expert judgement. There are many similar cases. In the fol-lowing pairs of examples the genus is perhaps doubtfully split off from its part-ner in parentheses *Limnas* (*Alopecurus*), *Eremopyrum* (*Agropyron*) and

*Lepturidium* (*Brachyachne*). Another interesting problem in this area is a recent suggestion which would change the names of most wheat species and their ancestors. Gupta and Baum (1989) present a summary of the arguments. Changes of names which result from genuine improvements in available information, and which therefore accurately reflect inter-species relationships are to be welcomed, since eventually other specialists do benefit. The problem is to know when proposed changes are properly justified.

## Species

What remains to be said about species? The number of species of course substantially exceeds that of genera (about 10,000 and 700 respectively). Additionally, many more taxonomists and other scientists are involved. Often they will be working with published floras in need of revision. Within these limitations a grass may be correctly identified according to the available flora even if in the light of more modern ideas the species or genus name needs to be changed. Sixty years ago, a student using Bentham and Hooker (1924) would have identified the reed as *Arundo phragmites* L. More recently, using Clapham, Tutin and Warburg (1952) the identity would be *Phragmites communis* Trin. whilst the third edition of the same flora (Clapham, Tutin and Moore, 1987) in which the nomenclature was adjusted to conform with the Flora Europea, gives the name as *Ph. australis* (Cav.) Trin. ex Steudel.

For the foreseeable future, especially in those countries where, until now, taxonomic coverage has been rather thin, we must expect continuing change not reluctantly but positively as it represents quickening interest and long overdue activity. New species continue to be described and especially in tropical countries with a rich grass flora this is likely to continue for many years yet. As with the decision to erect new genera, the decision to describe a new species remains a matter of informed judgement.

## Taxonomy and Evolution

Modern classifications of living organisms are expected to fulfil two functions. Firstly, they provide a means of identification and secondly, they reflect presumed evolutionary relationships. The first is eminently practical while the second is more speculative and it is an interesting feature of taxonomy that two such different aspects continue to interact. Both find expression when for example taxonomy becomes 'experimental' and by various means the relationship of presumably 'close' or 'less close' species are tested. The *Festuca* and *Lolium* situation mentioned previously provides one example.

The experimental testing of relationships finds practical application in plant breeding. For example, wild relatives of the major cereal species have provided cereal breeders with all manner of useful genes. The result is a proven technology that continues to contribute very significantly to the improvement of the world's grain crops.

In recent years this long established approach has been complemented by new developments in molecular biology. It has addressed such questions as whether plant breeding can be accelerated, gene function better understood and if the gene pool can be expanded by adding genetic material from 'remote' sources. It is worth stressing that all of this takes place against a taxonomic background which it is mistaken and inefficient to disregard. For an extended discussion of this area see, for wheat, Lagudah and Appels (1992); maize, Hoisington (1992) and for rice, Kochert (1992).

# Chorology

The systems of classification previously described use morphological similarities as evidence of relationship. Such systems are fundamental to plant science and unlikely to be replaced. Their traditional data can be augmented by information from anatomy, ecology, genetics and physiology leading to the multicharacter approach of Watson for example.

While utilising such approaches additional systems of classification can be developed and that for grasses, due to Clayton, will be briefly examined here.

Any tribe, subtribe, genus or species has a characteristic geographical distribution. Unrelated grasses, for example *Anthephora pubescens* and *Chloris gayana*, may share the same distribution. Extended search shows that a total of some 20 largely unrelated grasses also share the region defined as 'Sudano-Zambesian'. Groupings of grasses, some large, some small can be identified for other areas of the world and comprise 'phytochoria'. Any grouping will embrace a range of ecological habitats. Where a habitat is degraded and desertified reference to the appropriate phytochorion could indicate which species properly belong there. Theoretically, the persistence of these associations raises such questions as how they first came to be established and how is it that they continue to persist. For further information see Renvoize et al. (1992).

In recent years agrostologists have recognised not only a distinction between $C_3$ and $C_4$ but also that $C_4$ grasses exist in several forms. Eventually it came to be understood that photosynthetic variants followed taxonomic lines. The 'fit' was not complete, however, prompting both new physiology and taxonomic revision. (Reference has already been made to *Aristida* and *Stipagrostis*.) The next chapter indicates something of the profound changes that have occurred in our awareness of $C_3$ and especially $C_4$ mechanisms of photosynthesis.

# Chapter 6

# Photosynthetic Diversity

This chapter focuses on some aspects of photosynthesis which are associated with diversity among the grasses. For many years it has been known that photosynthesis in grasses includes both of the major biochemical pathways for carbon dioxide ($CO_2$) reduction: the so-called $C_3$ and $C_4$ pathways, whose bare outlines are indicated in Figures 6.1 and 6.2. The light-harvesting reactions of photosynthesis involving the initial absorption of light quanta by chlorophyll molecules, the release of oxygen from water, the production of the transient energy carrier

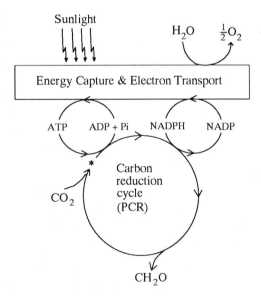

Figure 6.1. An outline of the photosynthetic carbon reduction cycle found in $C_3$ plants. The point marked * is the carboxylation reaction: ribulose bisphosphate + $CO_2$ produces phosphoglycerate: a 3-carbon compound, hence $C_3$ photosynthesis. Adapted from Robinson and Walker (1981).

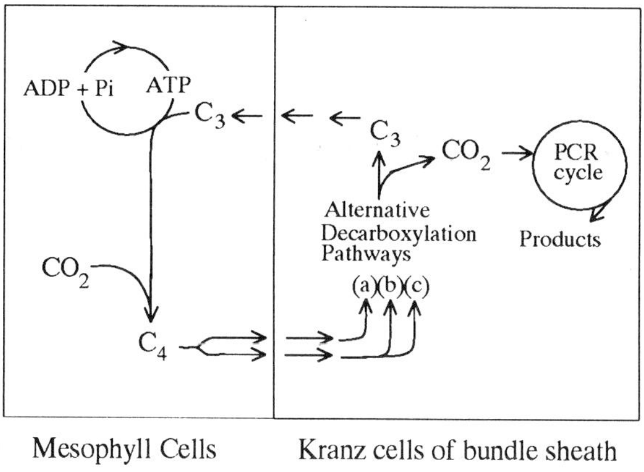

Mesophyll Cells          Kranz cells of bundle sheath

Figure 6.2. An outline of $C_4$ photosynthesis: $CO_2$ is taken up by mesophyll cells and incorporated into 4-carbon compounds (hence $C_4$). These compounds are translocated to bundle sheath cells where they are broken down (decarboxylated), by alternative pathways labelled a, b & c, and described in more detail in the text. The released $CO_2$ is then taken up by the conventional PCR cycle. Adapted and simplified from Edwards and Huber (1981).

adenosine triphosphate (ATP) and the reduced nicotinamide adenine dinucleotide (NADPH) are, so far as is known, the same in all grasses. The later stages, involving the reduction of carbon dioxide ($CO_2$) to carbohydrate differ between species. All species possess the so-called $C_3$ mechanism or PCR cycle shown in Figure 6.1. Some species, however, also possess an additional $C_4$ cycle shown in Figure 6.2. This operates as a temporary mechanism for $CO_2$ uptake, in which $CO_2$ is taken up through mesophyll cells to form organic acids with four carbon atoms which are then translocated to specialised bundle sheath cells and broken down to release $CO_2$ into the normal PCR cycle. The overall effect of this is to act as a 'CO_2 pump' which increases the effective concentration of $CO_2$ at its reaction site. The importance of this pump is that, in its absence, in $C_3$ species, a large proportion (up to one third) of the $CO_2$ absorbed in photosynthesis is lost immediately through the process of photorespiration. Increasing the effective $CO_2$ concentration on entry to the PCR cycle suppresses photorespiration and therefore increases the apparent photosynthetic rate.

There are three variants of the $C_4$ cycle, which differ in their intermediates and in their major decarboxylating enzymes. The initial uptake of $CO_2$ in $C_4$ species occurs throughout the leaf mesophyll. Its release and reincorporation into the PCR cycle is, however, restricted to specialised cells: the wreath or Kranz cells which surround each vascular bundle. $C_4$ species, therefore, have distinct anatomical features as well as distinct biochemical properties. Some $C_4$ species have a single layer of bundle sheath cells, whilst others have a second inner layer, the mestome sheath, adjacent to the metaxylem. A shorthand code for these two types is XyMS- and XyMS+ respectively.

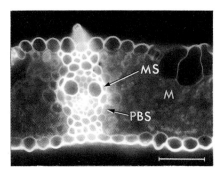

Figure 6.3. Transverse section of a *Triticum aestivum* leaf (typical pooid C₃). The vascular bundle has a parenchymatous bundle sheath outside a mestome sheath and many mesophyll cells separating adjacent veins. Bar = 50 μm.

In C₃ grass species the vascular bundles are surrounded by two layers of cells, neither of which is photosynthetic. Leaf mesophyll cells contain chloroplasts with well-developed grana capable of performing the complete PCR cycle of Figures 6.1 and 6.2. In typical pooid grasses (Figure 6.3), the mesophyll cells have fairly simple outlines, with scattered chloroplasts. In bamboos, in contrast, the cell outlines are much more complex, possessing highly characteristic 'arm' and 'fusoid' cells, and the chloroplasts are more prominent (Figure 6.4). These features may well have important physiological roles, but they are not associated with photosynthetic specialisation. In common with all C₃ plants, the first product after $CO_2$ incorporation is the 3-carbon compound phosphoglycerate. C₃ grasses predominate in cool regions of the world, but also occur in the tropics.

In C₄ species categorised as PEP-CK (synonyms PCK and PEP), the vascular bundles have Kranz anatomy, with bundle sheaths of two layers, coded as XyMS+. The outer layer is photosynthetic and contains chloroplasts arranged centrifugally (i.e. near the cell wall facing towards the outside of the vascular

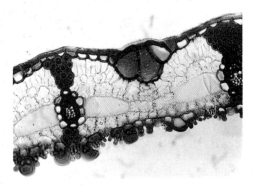

Figure 6.4. Transverse section of *Indocalamus tesselatus* leaf (C₃, bamboo). The characteristic, large 'fusoid' cells are seen either side of the vascular bundle, connected to the 'arm' cells: mesophyll cells with very irregular outlines.

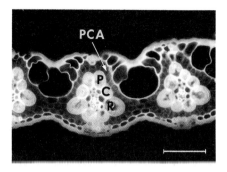

Figure 6.5. Transverse section of a *Sporobolus fimbriatus* leaf ($C_4$ PEP-CK). The main veins (not shown here) have a double-layered bundle-sheath, the outer layer with centrifugally oriented chloroplasts. Few mesophyll (PCA) cells separate adjacent veins. Bar = 100μm.

bundles, Figure 6.5). The chloroplast membranes form distinct grana. $CO_2$ is incorporated in leaf mesophyll cells forming oxaloacetate as the first ($C_4$) compound. This is converted to aspartate before being translocated to the bundle sheath cells. The major decarboxylating enzyme is the cytosolic phosphoenol pyruvate carboxylase and carbon skeletons are returned to the mesophyll as pyruvate or alanine. Representative species include *Brachiaria, Chloris, Panicum, Spartina* and *Zoysia,* grasses which grow in regions with both dry and wet seasons.

The NADP-ME version of the $C_4$ system has vascular bundles with Kranz anatomy but only a single layered bundle sheath (Figure 6.6), containing agranal $C_3$ chloroplasts arranged centrifugally and categorised as XyMS-. $CO_2$ taken into leaf mesophyll is combined with pyruvate to give the 4-carbon oxaloacetate which is then converted to malate. Malate is transported to the bundle sheath

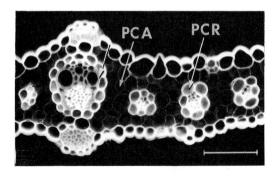

Figure 6.6. Section of *Panicum antidotale leaf* ($C_4$ NADP-ME). There are no intervening cells between the metaxylem vessels and the nearest PCR bundle sheath cells. Chloroplasts are centrifugally positioned in PCR cells, and there are few mesophyll (PCA) cells between adjacent vascular bundles. Bar = 100 μm.

cells and decarboxylated in the chloroplast by malate decarboxylase, using nicotinamide adenine dinucleotide phosphate as co-factor. The 3-carbon compound returned to the mesophyll is pyruvate. This mechanism is commoner in warm regions and representatives include *Saccharum, Zea* and *Sorghum* thus spanning a range of habitats from moist to semi-arid.

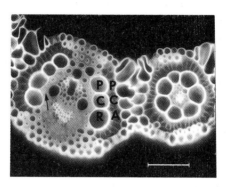

Figure 6.7. Transverse section of *Buchlöe dactyloides* leaf ($C_4$ NAD-ME). The arrow shows cells intervening between the metaxylem vessels and the photosynthetic (PCR) bundle sheath cells. Chloroplasts in the PCR cells are centrifugally oriented. There are few PCA cells between adjacent bundles. Bar = 100 μm.

$C_4$ species classed as NAD-ME again have vascular bundles with Kranz anatomy and a double layer of cells in the bundle sheath (Figure 6.7) and are therefore classed as XyMS+. The chloroplasts are granal and are arranged centripetally within the sheath cells. After $CO_2$ incorporation in the mesophyll, aspartate is again translocated into the bundle sheath, and then converted to malate before being decarboxylated in the mitochondria by malate decarboxylase using nicotinamide adenine dinucleotide as cofactor. $CO_2$ released by decarboxylation is fixed via the PCR cycle as before, and pyruvate or alanine returned to the mesophyll. This mechanism is also more common in warm regions and as rainfall decreases the proportion of NAD-ME type grasses in the flora increases. Representatives include *Buchloë, Cynodon, Eragrostis, Panicum, Sporobulus, Triodia* and *Triraphis*.

## $C_3/C_4$ Intermediates

*Panicum milioides*, possesses several characteristics which are 'intermediate' between $C_3$ and $C_4$. Anatomically it has a 'Kranz' double bundle sheath with centripetally placed chloroplasts reminiscent of NAD-ME types. Closer examination shows that its $C_3$ cycle is divided about one third in the mesophyll and two thirds in the bundle sheath (Rathnam and Chollet, 1980). More recently, the photosynthesis of a group of Australian grasses has been studied in three related genera: *Neurachne* ($C_3$, $C_4$, $C_3/C_4$), *Paraneurachne* ($C_4$) and *Thyridolepis* ($C_3$). Interesting features include the following. The $C_4$ representatives have a double layered sheath in the vascular bundle where the inner layer comprises the photo-synthetic layer and are thus XyMS-. The intermediate $C_3/C_4$ *Neurachne minor* has a bundle sheath appearance similar to its $C_4$ relative *N. munroi*. These grasses have an NADP-ME type $C_4$ mechanism although with few exceptions known to date, the vascular bundles of other such $C_4$ types are single sheathed. For a more detailed discussion see Hattersley and Watson (1992).

Although an attempt to investigate the genetics of $C_3$ and $C_4$ specialisation has been made within the Chenopodiaceae by crossing the $C_3$ species *Atriplex patula* with the $C_4$ *A. rosea*, no comparable example is known for grasses (Björkman et al., 1971).

# Recognition of Photosynthetic Alternatives

The anatomy of a leaf normally indicates its $C_3$ or $C_4$ status but exceptions do occur since the processes are primarily biochemical. Various alternative tests have been developed to discriminate between the processes.

## $\delta^{13}C$

$C_3$ plants discriminate against $^{13}CO_2$ relative to $^{12}CO_2$ but $C_4$ plants do not. The organic matter of $C_4$ plants therefore has a ratio of $^{13}C{:}^{12}C$ which is similar to that of the bulk atmosphere whilst that of $C_3$ plants is relatively depleted of $^{13}C$. The ratio is determined by burning dried plant material and measuring the pro-portions of $^{13}CO_2$ and $^{12}CO_2$ in comparison with an internationally agreed control. $\delta^{13}C$ is calculated as the proportionate change from this control, ex-pressed in parts per thousand. $C_3$ plants give lower values (-22 to -35) than $C_4$ plants (-9 to -18), and this is considered to be the most reliable way of distin-guishing between $C_3$ and $C_4$ types.

Using such tests, the $C_3/C_4$ intermediate *Neurachne minor* gives $\delta^{13}C$ values between those of *N. munroi* ($C_4$ ) and *N. tenuifolia* ($C_3$) and the intermediate *Panicum milioides* gives values below *P. bisculcatum* ($C_3$) (Hattersley et al., 1986).

### Photorespiration

This is detectable in $C_3$ grasses and is caused by ribulose bisphosphate combin-ing with oxygen rather than with $CO_2$. The eventual product is broken down by respiration, generating $CO_2$. Since this mechanism is only associated with photosynthesis, it is termed photorespiration. The lower the concentration of $CO_2$ in relation to $O_2$ the more likely is the latter to compete for the enzyme.

The synthesis of 4-carbon compounds uses the enzyme phosphoenol pyruvate carboxylase as the initial step and this incorporates $CO_2$ with no competitive influence of oxygen. When the 4-carbon compounds are broken down in the bundle sheath cells, the released $CO_2$ is present at a concentration higher than that which could be achieved by diffusion alone. Ribulose bisphosphate therefore reacts preferentially with $CO_2$ and not with $O_2$.

The major reason why the $C_4$ photosynthetic mechanism is superior to that of $C_3$, is that $C_4$ plants do not suffer the losses caused by photorespiration. One consequence of this is that $C_4$ plants have a lower $CO_2$ compensation point ($\Gamma$) of typically 0.1 - 0.4 $mmol.m^{-3}$ under bright light conditions than that of $C_3$ species which give a value of $\Gamma$ of 2 - 4 $mmol.m^{-3}$. This difference offers another means of distinguishing $C_3/C_4$ types. The technique is particularly useful for rapid screening in the field, since leaf samples can be enclosed in a glass vial or flask which also contains a dilute solution of sodium or potassium bicarbonate together with a pH indicator. The pH of the solution equilibrates with the $CO_2$ concentration of the surrounding air sufficiently well to discriminate $C_3$ from $C_4$ (Coombs, 1985). An interesting demonstration of the effect is to enclose seedlings of both $C_4$ and $C_3$ species in an airtight, illuminated container such as a bell-jar. The $C_4$ plant should grow at the expense of the $C_3$.

### Post-illumination burst, PIB

When an illuminated leaf is transferred to dark conditions, it evolves $CO_2$ at a high rate for about two minutes. The effect increases in magnitude with temperature. This is viewed as a remnant of photorespiration in $C_3$ plants that continues for a short period. PIB is absent from NADP-ME $C_4$ species, but NAD-ME and PEP-CK species show a burst which, unlike that from $C_3$ species, is not sensitive to oxygen concentration. It is interpreted as non-productive breakdown of the unused $C_4$ intermediates.

### The relative efficiencies of $C_3$ and $C_4$ photosynthesis

The best wheat ($C_3$) is about half the best sugar cane ($C_4$) performance in terms of carbon fixed per hectare but avoidance of photorespiration (which can lose up to 40% of fixed carbon) is only one factor in this comparison.

Sugar cane grows at lower latitudes with higher irradiance and could not match wheat at high latitudes. If the two species are to be properly compared, in what environment should it be done? Tropical grasses perform poorly in temperate environments and vice versa. Particular $C_4$ grasses may be more heat or cold adapted as may $C_3$ grasses. Additionally, it should be recognised that dry matter accumulation is not simply the outcome of photosynthetic efficiency. It can reflect length of growing season, performance in a suboptimal environment, the effect of leaf ageing or the partitioning of assimilates between competing sources and sinks (see Hay and Walker, 1989).

## The Evolution of $C_4$ Photosynthesis in Grasses

Three evolutionary trends, very approximately in step can be discerned among grasses. These are 'advancing' morphology, decline in basic chromosome number (though punctuated by polyploidy) and, in low latitude grasses, the adoption of various forms of $C_4$ photosynthesis. The generally accepted view of evolution amongst subfamilies suggest that they radiated from a common hypothetical ancestor (indicated by the asterisk in Figure 6.8). The distribution of photosynthetic mechanisms agrees fairly well with this view (Hattersley and Watson, 1992). $C_4$ photosynthesis is unknown in bamboos and the Pooideae and is commoner

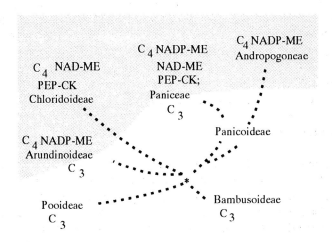

Figure 6.8. Photosynthetic taxonomy in the Poaceae (compiled from Clayton and Renvoize, 1986 and Prendergast and Hattersley, 1987).

among the more derived grasses. Since there is more than one kind of $C_4$ photosynthesis among the grasses the question arises as to whether they arose independently or could be placed in a derivative series, for grasses showing a sufficiently close relationship, to suggest a single origin and subsequent diversification. At present independent origins seem perhaps more likely but it is an open question.

$C_3$ species of grasses and all other families occur in all latitudes. Some supposed 'advanced' families, the Poaceae and perhaps 15 others include $C_4$ representatives virtually all in tropical or subtropical environments. Since, taxonomically within the grasses distribution is to some extent 'spotty' could the $C_4$ variants have evolved independently in response to the emergence of a post-Cretaceous 'tropical' environment? Evidence continues to accumulate that among $C_4$ grasses the NADP-ME malate formers occur more in wet situations whilst the NAD-ME malate formers are found in arid environments and the PEP-CK aspartate formers are intermediate (see Hattersley, 1992). This adaptation to environment may help to explain some of the anomalies of taxonomic distribution of which the following are examples.

*Panicum* with about 500 species, and therefore one of the largest grass genera, has $C_3$ and all $C_4$ types, whilst different species of *Leptochloa* are either PEP-CK or NAD-ME showing that the different mechanisms can occur among close relatives. In contrast, the NADP-ME type is found in genera as dissimilar as *Aristida* (Arundinoid), *Axonopus* and *Zea* (contrasted Panicoids). Variation within a single species is possible since *Alloteropsis semi-alata* is PEP-CK in Australia but of two South African ecotypes, one is $C_3$ and the other NADP-ME. Similarly, *Bouteloua curtipendula* possesses two mechanisms, PEP-CK and NAD-ME which can co-exist within a single plant. Is this exceptional? Closer examination shows that plants characterised primarily as NAD-ME aspartate-formers lack detectable activity by NADP-ME and PEP-CK enzyme systems. These grasses include *Eleusine corocana* and *Panicum miliaceum*. Conversely, both NADP-ME types such as *Bouteloua curtipendula*, already mentioned, and *Chloris gayana, Eriochloa borumensis* and *Panicum maximum* show appreciable NAD-ME activity (Rathnam and Chollet, 1980).

*Neurachne minor* is (within the mesophyll) both $C_3$ and $C_4$ NADP-ME. In summary, therefore, one species can be represented in different $C_4$ ecotypes or can run two $C_4$ mechanisms simultaneously or can run in the mesophyll both $C_3$ and $C_4$ together.

Anatomically there are also challenging problems. NADP-ME types typically have a single-layered bundle sheath (XyMS-). This $C_4$ mechanism is biochemically consistent among Arundinoid grasses where it occurs, but two genera, *Eriachne* and *Pheidochloa*, have double-layered sheaths (XyMS+). By contrast, no NAD-ME is known with a single sheath.

**Past, present and future**

Hattersley and Watson (1992) have endeavoured to relate alternative photosynthetic pathways to past climatic change. Since global warming is at least a possibility, and in any case levels of atmospheric $CO_2$ have been rising for more than a century, might grasses eventually undergo further evolution in response to these changes? Alternatively, as scientists come better to understand photosynthesis might they not seek deliberately to modify it? We do not know, but already grasses provide us with contrasted model systems.

# Chapter 7

# Reproductive Diversity

An initial assumption might be that a diploid grass operating under the influence of the SZ incompatibility system generating seeds annually was the norm for the Poaceae. In reality there are numerous departures from this pattern. It should be recognised that these departures can be seen in two ways. Firstly and most obviously they reflect part of present day grass diversity but secondly such mechanisms of change have themselves evolved. If therefore, for example, we wished to examine the effects of apomixis sooner or later we ought to consider, too, what caused the apomixis itself. Before however exploring these questions it will be appropriate to examine some other themes in grass evolution.

## Chromosome number in the Poaceae

Two trends are discernible in the Poaceae. One is a decline in basic number from the bamboos (12) and arundinoids (12) toward arguably the more modern grasses with pooids (7) chloridoids (9) and panicoids (9). In these more modern groups there are individual genera where this trend has gone to an extreme. In the Pooideae, *Airopsis* $x = 4$ and *Zingeria* $x = 2$ whilst in the Panicoideae, *Iseiloma* $x = 3$. Such a stepwise loss of chromosomes can be read as an ecological specialisation that is accompanied by the shedding of superfluous DNA.

Superimposed upon this first trend is a second, namely the incidence of polyploidy. At its simplest, if two ecologically specialised diploids hybridise and double the chromosome number a resulting fertile allotetraploid might be expected to combine the ecological adaptability of both species. Since about 70 per cent of grass species are polyploid the global success of the Poaceae can probably, to some extent, be explained in this way.

A further consideration is that nucleotide sequences within a chromosome can be repeated many times yet despite this do not have a detectable coding function. Such blocks of nucleotides appear to have, in the course of evolution, been replicated and retained within the chromosome. Such a process is known as amplification. Deletion events are also possible. Among wheats the phenomenon of amplification has been studied in great detail but its significance remains unclear. For references see Flavell et al. (1987) and Lagudah and Appels (1992).

A peculiarity, so far unexplained, about the SZ incompatibility system in grasses is that it is not disrupted by polyploidy, a situation that contrasts with gametophytic incompatibility systems elsewhere. However, even though the SZ system remains intact, polyploidy can both disrupt orderly chromosome pairing at meiosis leading to infertility and provide an opportunity for normal sexual reproduction to be replaced by apomixis.

### Cleistogamy

The SZ system would on theoretical grounds be expected to maintain heterozygosity through succeeding generations and to operate against persistent self-fertilisation. However, in many grasses cleistogamy occurs. Such automatic self-fertilisation can only succeed if the SZ system is somehow undermined or discarded. Cleistogamy is normal in wheat but any inbreeding depression that might result has not prevented this crop from becoming the world's most important cereal - a situation that confronts us with a paradox.

## Need a Grass Set Seed?

The chapter began with the assumption that seed production was a necessary and regular occurrence. Is this always the case? Why should not a grass plant simply vegetate indefinitely once it is established? *Panicum turgidum* and *Stipagrostis pungens* are but two of many examples from semi-desert conditions where seed production can occur but propagation is commonly vegetative.

Some bamboos flower and seed frequently but others have long vegetative periods of up to a century or even more. There is then a mass flowering described either as 'synchronous' or 'mast' flowering as reviewed in detail by Janzen (1976). The flowering of bamboo populations and their temporary decline has, of course, serious implications for survival of the giant panda. As commonly perceived, bamboos replicate vegetatively and seed formation is rare.

An interesting and in some ways more extreme case concerns the pasture grass *Festuca rubra*. Seed formation occurs here but given the establishment of a sward many individuals will die out and relatively few long lived individuals, by vegetative reproduction, come to dominate the population. Such individuals may, it is estimated, be up to 600 years old. For *F. ovina*, a comparable situation probably occurs (Harberd, 1961; 1962).

A further case is that of *Phragmites australis*, the reed, where despite prolific flowering seed production is virtually unknown and propagation seems exclusively vegetative. In view of the large areas covered and the continuity of habitation it has been suggested that some clones may be several thousand years old. See Richards (1990).

For ephemeral grasses dependence on seed reproduction is total but clearly there are interesting departures from this pattern as shown by the foregoing examples and each of them contributes different models to the study of grass population genetics. For practical purposes we can classify plants as annual or perennial but some of the latter under stress of very dry years can behave as annuals. By contrast pearl millet is described as an annual but in practice it is one that can in some ways mimic a perennial in its ability by going dormant to withstand heat and drought stress and resume active growth when conditions improve.

## Replacing the seed

The previous section explored some of the ways in which dependence on the seed might be diminished but behind it lay the assumption that seed reproduction remained an option. Even this need not be so since the spikelet can be replaced by a small plantlet formed in its stead. This is called prolifery or vivipary and is known in numerous grasses. Figure 4.12 illustrated prolifery in *Brachiaria decumbens,* and a variant of *Festuca ovina* quite commonly reproduces in this way, as shown in Figure 2.12.

There is however a yet more searching question to be asked. If the seed habit is retained is it what we think it is or is it a means of vegetative reproduction merely masquerading as a seed?

## Redefining the seed

The grass seed is normally shed with the fruit, the whole structure known as a 'caryopsis'. That much is a commonplace to any student of grasses. Within the caryopsis, the seed that corresponds with botanical definition rather than practical requirement, is assumed to result from normal double fertilisation described earlier in Chapter 3. In many cases what we expect to happen does so but an interesting and important group of exceptions exist referred to as apomicts or plants manifesting apomixis. Mechanisms can vary but the essential point is that seed formation by-passes double fertilisation and represents one more and peculiar form of vegetation reproduction. The apomictic seed is thus a vegetative propagule quite indistinguishable from sexually produced seed except by a detailed study.

# Apomixis

Originally, the term apomixis implied any form of non-sexual reproduction. It was subdivided into two categories - vegetative reproduction and agamospermy, the latter implying non-sexual reproduction via the seed. More recently 'agamospermy' has been largely discarded and the term apomixis substituted.

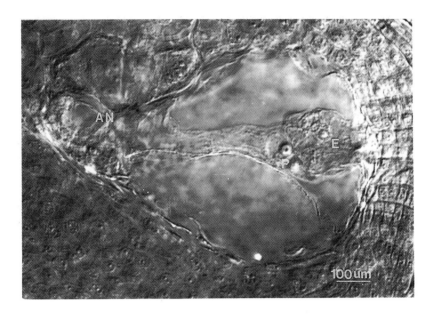

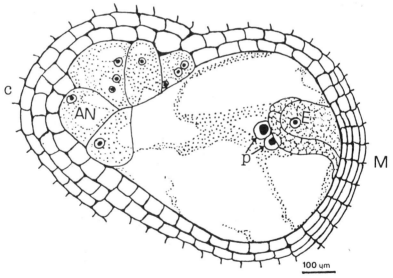

Figure 7.1 (above) and 7.2 (opposite) illustrate the use of interference microscopy to study aspects of plant structure. In this technique (adapted from Young et al., 1979), the tissue is cleared and viewed through optics which reveal a thin 'optical section' within the specimen: in this case an ovule. The advantage of the technique is that sequential planes can be viewed to give a three-dimensional impression of the whole. In each figure the photograph shows a single plane through the ovule whilst the drawing shows an interpretation which may have been derived from several adjacent planes.

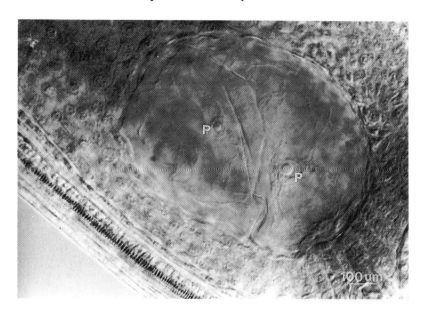

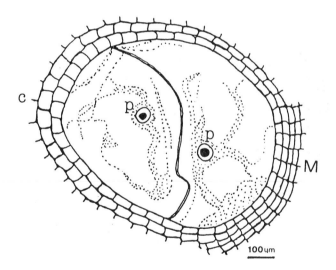

Figure 7.1 (opposite) shows a sexual embryo sac obtained from an open pollinated F₂ plant of a cross between the tetraploid *Pennisetum glaucum* (2n = 28) and the hexaploid *P. squamulatum* (2n = 54) showing a single sexual embryo sac within the ovule with proliferated antipodals (AN), two polar nuclei (P) and an egg apparatus (E). M shows the micropyle region and C the chalazal region.

Figure 7.2 (above) shows two apomictic embryo sacs within the same ovule of *P. squamulatum*, each showing one polar nucleus (P).

Here the term apomixis is used in its more recent sense and refers only to the modification of the seed.

Apomixis can now be subdivided into two categories 'diplospory' and 'apospory'. In the first case the megaspore mother cell does not usually undergo meiosis but instead, via mitosis, will give rise to four diploid megaspores of which one will be functional. This occurs in *Elymus*, *Eragrostis* and *Nardus* for example. Apospory (far more common than diplospory among grasses) occurs when a nucellar cell becomes elaborated as a diploid embryo sac. Such aposporous embryo sacs can occur as multiples with a given ovule and they may exist alongside a normal sexual embryo sac derived in the usual way from a megaspore.

Typically, an aposporous embryo sac arises as follows. A diploid nucleus divides twice to give a four nucleate embryo sac. The nuclei then rearrange to give an egg, two synergids and one polar nucleus. In this condition the embryo sac is primed for further development. Note that the embryo sac derived in this way is devoid of antipodals, a feature that provides a convenient point of discrimination between sexual and apomictic cases. Figures 7.1 and 7.2 illustrate contrasting sexual and asexual embryo sacs in *Pennisetum*.

**Fertilisation in apomicts**

Fertilisation may or may not occur. For a discussion of this point see Chapman (1971) with regard to the genus *Dichanthium*. Fertilisation should be understood as that situation where both male gametes are functional, one fusing with the egg and one with the two polar nuclei. A modification of true fertilisation we consider next is 'pseudogamy'.

**Pseudogamy**

One of the two male gametes delivered by the pollen tube, that approaching the egg, contributes neither cytoplasm nor nucleus. The (unreduced) egg therefore remains diploid. The haploid male gamete approaching the central cell does function and its union with the single, diploid polar nucleus yields a triploid primary endosperm nucleus. The peculiarity of pseudogamy is that it mimics sexual fusion of an eight nucleate embryo sac and in both cases a diploid egg is associated with triploid endosperm. This statement does, however, need qualification. Apomixis, almost without exception, is confined to polyploids, and so the diploid/triploid situation just described requires the appropriate multiples of chromosome number. Of course, not all polyploids are apomicts.

Not all apomicts are pseudogamous and examples without this process occur in *Cortaderia* and probably *Danthonia*. Removal of stigmas before anthesis, by preventing pollination, would also preclude pseudogamy. If apomixis were known to occur and did so in the absence of stigmas, this is evidence for non-pseudogamous and therefore 'autogamous' apomixis.

**The significance of apomixis**

Clearly if an organism reproduces indefinitely by apomixis, it precludes advantageous recombination via meiosis and syngamy. Even a rare sexual event allows genetic change. Apomixis is thus something of an enigma, but if we assume the 'facultative' situation, where occasional genetic change can occur, it is a mechanism for perpetuating unchanged genotypes showing hybrid vigour. *Cenchrus ciliaris* has been introduced into Australia within the last 150 years and is, recognisably, a successful new entrant to parts of the Australian flora probably functioning as a facultative apomict. By contrast *C. ciliaris* has disappeared from large parts of the southern Sahara during prolonged drought. Could we assume therefore that facultative apomixis is good but not that good and that ultimately deterioration of the Sahel proved too severe for its survival?

**A further enigma**

Virtually without exception all grass apomicts are polyploid but all grass polyploids are not apomicts. Put differently, apomixis seems only to function and express itself at the polyploid level. There appears therefore to be something inherently conducive about polyploidy toward apomixis. No completely satisfactory explanation is available. For discussion see Chapman (1992a).

An important consideration is that among facultative apomicts a swing toward increased sexuality appears to be under seasonal influence in *Dichanthium aristatum* (Knox, 1967) suggesting that apomixis is a subtle and sophisticated adaptation at least for this species and possibly for others, including *Pennisetum* illustrated earlier.

In other cases, polyploids have been shown to have a disrupted meiosis and to be apomictic. In such cases apomixis by-passes a meiosis that would lead to sterility and provides an alternative route to seed production. Apomixis is thus seen in such cases as a 'salvage' operation. What such a description overlooks is that the potential for apomixis was already present in the genotype and whether any present salvage function is not a diversion from its earlier and original one toward which any seasonal responsiveness might be a pointer.

# Outbreeding

Cleistogamy (implying a non-functional SZ incompatibility system) makes for inbreeding and apomixis, by a different means, provides a restriction of genetic exchange. The emphasis hitherto in this discussion has been on mechanisms that tend to protect existing genetic arrangements. Suppose however that sexual reproduction were not only the norm but that additionally the plants were further modified so as to yield in each generation recombinant individuals with self-fertilisation as a relatively rare event.

Clearly, an incompatibility system makes for outbreeding. Connor (1979) has shown that self-incompatibility occurs widely among grasses but experimental evidence for the SZ system, unique to grasses, is fully confirmed in less than a dozen species so far, all of them pooid grasses. If a grass floret were to depart from being hermaphrodite, self-fertilisation within a flower would no longer be possible. If both sexes were present within the same spikelet, however, self-fertilisation might still be possible. Separation of the sexes to different areas of the same plant (monoecy) or to different plants (dioecy), in contrast, provides an effective mechanism to restrict or even prevent self-fertilisation.

Monoecious grasses of which nearly 50 genera are known include *Coix*, *Distichlis*, *Tripsacum* and *Zea*. Dioecy, here as in most other plants, is less common than monoecy, and includes species of *Buchloë*, *Cortaderia*, *Sohnsia*, *Spinifex* and *Zygochloa*. It should be recognised that the distinction between monoecy and dioecy need not be clear cut. A sample of *Buchloë dactyloides* seed can yield both monoecious and dioecious individuals and many years ago Jones (1934) showed that a quite simple genetic change could, under controlled conditions, cause *Zea mays* to become and remain dioecious. *Distichlis*, too, can be either monoecious or dioecious. For illustrations of monoecious and dioecious grasses see Chapter 4.

**Bamboo tissue culture - a new option**

Recently it has been found that seeds of bamboo grown in vitro under the right conditions can flower and seed after several months rather than after several decades. First reported by Nadgauda et al. (1990) and Hanke (1990), other workers have begun to find similar results. If this can be made routine, the consequences would be momentous, since it would substantially enhance the prospects for bamboo improvement through breeding as well as for the study of its reproductive physiology.

# Chapter 8

# Grasses in Cultivation

From time to time off types occur in grasses as in other plants. Some oddities are quite pleasing in appearance and attract the attention of horticulturists. Leaf variegation occurs in several grasses that have become ornamentals, including *Arundo donax*, *Deschampsia cespitosa*, *Molinia caerulea*, *Phalaris canariensis* and *Miscanthus sinesis* among others. Off types among grasses fall into two categories as follows:

*1. Chimaeras* – These are genetic changes that do not occur in the germ line. That is to say, a variant is produced involving a patch of tissue that may develop into a branching leafy stem or tiller and be used to propagate vegetatively the off type.

*2. Mutants* – These are genetic variants often segregating in a Mendelian fashion and including features such a free-threshing and non-shattering which have played a key role in the process of domestication.

## Chimaeras

It is perhaps among the bamboos that the greatest range of grass chimaeras is to be found. These, having once occurred, have then been propagated vegetatively. The following is a small selection from among these variants.

*Arundinaria viridistriata*: an ornamental, hardy under temperate conditions with yellow and green-striped leaves. This condition is by no means confined to this species (Figure 8.1).

*Bambusa ventricosa*: the so-called 'Buddha's belly' form, where the base of the internode is bulbous (Figure 8.2). A miniature version is produced by growing the plant under 'bonsai' conditions. (A variant of *Phyllostachys aurea* shows bulges at the *tops* of each internode.)

Figure 8.1. Variegated leaves of
*Arundinaria viridistriata.*

Figure 8.2. The 'Buddha's belly' form of
stem of *Bambusa ventricosa.*

Figure 8.3. Variegated leaves and stems
of *Bambusa vulgaris* var. *striata.*

Figure 8.4. Variegated leaves and stems
of *Phyllostachys bambusoides.*

*Bambusa vulgaris* var. *striata*: a variant found growing to five or six metres tall,
that is planted as a tropical ornamental. Both stem and leaves are striped green
and white (Figure 8.3).

*Phyllostachys bambusoides*: an important source of cane in China and Japan.
Among its variants are '*subvariegata*' with green-striped leaf blades and
'*castellonii*' with alternating green stripes on its otherwise yellow internodes
(Figure 8.4). *P. aurea*, curiously, provides a variant '*flavescens-inversa*' with
yellow stripes on its otherwise green internodes.

Figure 8.5. Stems of *Phyllostachys edulis* and *Chimonobambusa quadrangularis* with square cross-sections.

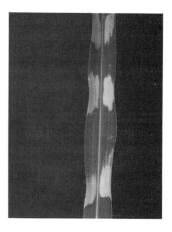

Figure 8.6. Horizontal variegation in the leaf of *Miscanthus sinensis*.

Figure 8.7. Longitudinal leaf variegation in *Phalaris canariensis*.

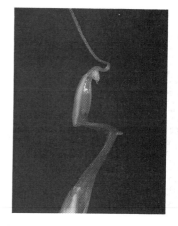

Figure 8.8. 'Hooded' mutant affecting the lemma and awn of barley.

*P. edulis:* provides 50% of the Chinese bamboo forest and is a source of both timber and edible bamboo shoots. Among its numerous variants is '*heterocycla*' or 'tortoiseshell' bamboo where alternate internodes bulge in opposite directions.

**Other bamboo variants**

The status of some other bamboo variants is more doubtful and the long intervals between flowering in many cases precludes their genetic study. Mention can be made of *Pleioblastus gramineus* where the internodes have a curious spiral arrangement and *Chimonobambusa quadrangularis* where the stems have a square cross-section (the smaller section of Figure 8.5). Both of these could be either mutants or chimaeras. *C. quadrangularis* is especially interesting since it can be mimicked in *Phyllostachys edulis,* for example, by enclosing the young stem primordium in square shuttering so that the enclosed culm is forced into a square cross-section as it grows (the larger section of Figure 8.5).

Chimaeras both in bamboo and in other grasses have in recent years become widely used among horticulturalists and there is no doubt that they provide a valued ingredient in garden design that harmonises well with other plants that are grown whether for flowers or foliage (Figures 8.6 and 8.7). Many grasses are drought tolerant and some of these ornamentals are useful therefore where gardening is hampered by water shortages.

# Mutants

The list of mutants among the grasses runs into thousands. Many of them have curiosity status, although they can also have some use in plotting linkage relationships. To illustrate something of the range of form, examples are given from *Hordeum, Sorghum* and *Zea.*

*Hordeum* produces several well-known morphological mutants. Its normally lax inflorescence can be transformed to the upright 'erectoid' form. 'Hooded' is a remarkable modification of the awn that can take several forms depending on the particular genetic background (Figure 8.8). *Hordeum* can exist in normal or 'naked' forms where in the latter case the lemma and the palea are not adherent to the caryopsis. Again, the lodicules may or may not inflate. In the former case (the 'abnormal' one for barley) inflated lodicules open the floret and permit cross-pollination for an otherwise self-pollinated crop.

*Sorghum* sometimes segregates a mutant known as 'goose-neck' (Figure 8.9). This inverts the inflorescence and in combination with prominent awns has been advocated as a method of countering the depredations of *Quelea* birds by making it marginally more awkward for them to perch on a ripe inflorescence. This may function when the birds are given a choice of forms to attack, but would probably be ineffective in a pure stand of goose-neck forms.

Variation in maize raises some fundamental questions and these are discussed in a later section.

Figure 8.9. 'Goose-neck' mutant of *Sorghum*.

Figure 8.10. Fragile mature panicle of *Saccharum*.

## Domestication

Cultivation of grass chimaeras concerns a minority of people. Cereal culture is quite different in that millions of people are farmers and millions more, indeed almost everyone else, are consumers. The contrast, though, is not merely one of scale. Domestication of cereals is, arguably, an evolutionary process begun some thousands of years ago and engendered by the new and special needs of humankind. Cereal domestication depends not on chimaeras but on mutants and changes to crops from their wild relatives are highly heritable.

The study of domestication, whether of plants or of animals, involves a wide range of disciplines including archaeology, ecology, genetics, physiology and taxonomy. Individually, domestication of the major cereals has been treated in numerous accounts, see for example wheat (Evans and Peacock, 1981; Lupton, 1987), maize (Galinat, 1983) and rice (Chang, 1976; Oka, 1988). For references to the minor cereals see Harlan (1992) and de Wet (1992).

Our aim here is not to describe particular cereals in detail but to concentrate on some issues which are general to cereal domestication. Some reference will however be made to bread wheat, maize and rice.

Wild grasses have adherent chaff surrounding the grain, and the inflorescence fragments when mature (Figure 8.10). In this way, protected caryopses are dispersed. When the first wild grasses were domesticated, two important changes commonly occurred: namely the grain become easily separated from the chaff (free-threshing) and the inflorescence lost the ability to fragment and became non-shattering. Free-threshing and non-shattering are the mutant forms that underlie the evolution of cereals and they are the forms that Neolithic farmers consciously or unconsciously selected.

**A perspective.** Grasses as members of the Angiosperms have probably existed for about 70,000,000 years evolving during the Cretaceous and with various changes thereafter. Against this background the invention of agriculture, and with it the domestication of cereals, is relatively recent beginning probably about 10,000 years ago or roughly twice the interval of time that the earliest inscribed clay tablets have survived or put differently about 1/7000th of the time that grasses have existed.

Precisely why agriculture should have begun is uncertain but an increase in human numbers combined with a decrease in available food that could be obtained from hunting and gathering may have been the principle triggers. Curiously, the appropriate conditions seem to have existed at about the same time in both the New and the Old Worlds. Since we assume no contact between the separated populations of each hemisphere we assume, too, their independent agricultural origins. On present evidence these began in Central America and the Near East. From these two origins (and perhaps others) agriculture was adopted elsewhere with of course appropriate choices among suitable existing or introduced plants.

It is sometimes inferred that the origins of agriculture were almost an unconscious process leading to a reliable food supply that permitted urbanisation, settled societies and the beginning of an artistic and technological tradition. It is perhaps more realistic to see agriculture as a conscious part of the creative process rather than its dull and unwitting precursor. It is insufficiently recognised that evidence for irrigated agriculture is almost as old as agriculture itself implying some level of conscious organisation by a relatively cohesive society.

**The choice of cereals.** In the Near East wheat and barley were domesticated and have remained so although later it will be necessary to specify more clearly what is meant by 'wheat'. Some time later, in Northern Europe and elsewhere rye and oats were added. In China proso millet and foxtail millet were domesticated though later largely superseded by rice (de Wet, 1992). In the Americas a foxtail millet was cultivated early but about 7000 years ago was largely replaced by maize. Wheat, maize, rice and to some extent barley thus emerged early as preferred cereals and have retained and strengthened their pre-eminence to the present day. Apart from these examples there are numerous other cereals that were domesticated as agriculture spread and have remained, since then, continuously in cultivation. The choices Neolithic farmers made have thus proved very durable.

**Wheat.** Nowadays wheat, that is to say 'bread wheat', forms the centrepiece of world agriculture. It is the world's most important cereal, is economically highly significant since it enters conspicuously into trade between countries and it draws and indeed shapes many of the fundamental aspects of modern cereal science. By any standards it is a remarkable crop being both productive and widely adapted. This situation attracted the attention of Pliny a Roman historian and John Ray (1704) a famous and discerning eighteenth century naturalist among others. Bread wheat is but one of several wheats which, curiously, was unknown to the first agriculturalists, since it evolved at a later time. Uncertainties exist since carbonised (prehistoric) grains cannot be unequivocally identified, but an outline of events can be conjectured as follows.

*Triticum monococcum* exists in two forms, subspp. *boeoticum* and *monococcum*, respectively wild and cultivated variants. One or other of these diploids (2n=14) hybridised with some related diploid, and the hybrid doubled its chromosomes to produce the tetraploid, wild species *T. dicoccoides* from which *T. dicoccum* emerged as the domesticated variant. At some point (uncertain as to either time or place) one of these tetraploids hybridised naturally with a third diploid variously known as *Aegilops squarrosa* or *T. tauschii*. The resulting hybrid again doubled its chromosomes to create the hexaploid *T. aestivum*. The role of *Ae. squarrosa* is critical since with it came gluten, the protein that adds elasticity to dough and permits leavened bread to rise through its retention of bubbles of carbon dioxide generated by the yeast.

Could the archaeological record help to reveal the approximate place and time at which bread wheat first appeared? Cereal grains occur at archaeological sites as carbonised grains but it is difficult to identify whether or not a particular sample is emmer or bread wheat because of the close similarity of appearance. The origin of bread wheat, this immensely important event, remains therefore tantalisingly beyond our grasp but we believe it to have been in the 'Near East' and to have been *after* the dawn of agriculture.

**Rice.** This common name can be applied to several recognisably different species and which represent independent agricultural traditions. These include *Oryza glaberrima* domesticated from *O. barthii* in W. Africa, *Zizania aquatica* in N. America perhaps best regarded as a semi-domesticate and *O. sativa* derived from *O. nivara* in several parts of the Orient independently and represented by '*indica*', '*japonica*' and '*javanica*' rices. *O. sativa* now provides the bulk of the world's rice crop, the others increasingly a minority.

**Minor cereals.** Among the ancient Greeks it was to the goddess Demeter (Ceres to the Romans) that the gift of agriculture was attributed. A detail of the story is that to Triptolemus, Demeter was indebted since he first revealed to her the whereabouts of her lost daughter Persephone who had been abducted by Zeus, king of the Gods and held captive in the Underworld. In gratitude Triptolemus was given a gift of 'corn' and a winged chariot so that he might spread agriculture around the world. Corn here should not be understood as maize since it was unknown to Greek civilisation but would have been an Old World cereal such as wheat or barley. What is of special interest here is the Greek recognition of agriculture originating in one place and being adopted elsewhere. There is a host of cereals derived from indigenous wild grasses presumably in response to a situation where a technology could be imported but not its raw material. Thus the migrating Cushites are believed, some 3000 years ago, to have domesticated sorghum in Ethiopia as it became evident to them that wheat was unproductive in their new environment.

There remains the problem of how far particular domestications are genuinely independent. Pearl millet originating from wild *Pennisetum* could be either an innovative development in Africa or could have been based on what was done with other grasses elsewhere.

The minor cereals include dozens of species but attitudes toward them vary. Many of them have attracted little science beyond taxonomic recognition and consequently they remain outside the mainstream of agricultural development. Alternatively, it is recognised that in a hungry world they remain useful resources that should not be ignored. An interesting example is provided by *Eragrostis tef* (t'ef). This is a small seeded grass sometimes included among the millets. It provides a hay crop in several countries but is eaten only in Ethiopia for its seeds where it is the principal cereal and greatly esteemed there. With the coming of scientific agriculture official policy there was to neglect t'ef in favour of wheat, maize, barley and sorghum where highly developed technology was already available. Gradually, it was recognised that the local Ethiopian taste preferences mattered sufficiently to generate t'ef research and slowly the situation has changed.

It does not follow that nothing can be done for these rather obscure crops notwithstanding the momentum of development behind the major cereals. A practical problem is to judge whether or not some hitherto minor cereal genuinely has potential for improvement or is, despite serious effort by scientists, unlikely to be improved.

**Genetic conservation.** A generally definable pattern to emerge in the twentieth century has been the recognition of close relationships between cultivated cereals and their wild relatives. From this it has been a short step to utilise such relatives in plant breeding programmes. This in turn has led to the accumulation of extensive collections described as 'gene banks' or germ plasm stores. Such collections nowadays go well beyond cereal or other crop plant relatives because of a general concern with conservation of threatened species.

Judged by the scale of existing collections, the germ plasm requirements of breeders seem unlikely to be exhausted in the foreseeable future. The same is probably true of the minor cereals where collection has been extensive and the number of active breeders small. The need to conserve genetic material has been very actively pursued and has now become something of a conditioned reflex. It is perhaps necessary now to ask more critical questions about whether gene banks are too large or too small and to what extent the stored material can retain its long term viability and be effectively exploited. A more significant point to recognise is that as humankind collects, documents, stores and eventually exploits this lengthening list of species, domestication itself becomes an all embracing concept. The idea of human 'dominion' over all living things set out in the book of Genesis seems almost to have become today's routine scientific policy. As for 'domestication' it is hardly accurate any longer to confine the term, without qualification, to farm animals and traditionally cultivated crops.

**The rate of domestication.** A question considered more recently in considerable detail is how long does it take, or how many generations does a wild grass require, to become changed to a cultivated cereal. For an authoritative account see Davies and Hillman (1992).

## The Maize Inflorescence

Perhaps the most thought-provoking of all grass changes occur in maize inflorescences. At first sight the familiar monoecious growth habit with female silks about halfway up and male tassels placed terminally seems consistent enough from one field to another. Closer inspection shows a remarkable situation. Infestation of the tassels by frit fly (*Oscinella frit*) causes hypertrophy of the vestigial ovary and pseudograins develop among the male spikelets (Figure 8.11). Even severe drought stress is occasionally sufficient to induce true grain formation in the tassels. Finally, a range of genetic mutants that cause 'tassel seeding' has been known for many years (Figure 8.12).

How are we to regard these changes in maize that make the familiar growth habit seem rather less rigidly determined than we had supposed? One approach is to recognise that present day maize is the outcome of about 6 or 7000 years of domestication - not long in evolutionary terms but, significantly, resulting in

Figure 8.11. *Oscinella frit* attack on maize, causing tassels to bear pseudograins.

Figure 8.12. Tassel seeded mutant of maize.

cultivars that have changed relative to their wild progenitors far more conspicuously than is the case for wheat or barley. Of all cereal crops, maize could most be regarded as a 'man-made artefact'. For example, the grains are 'naked' protruding well above the reduced glumes, lemma and palea, although 'pod' forms, where these organs cover the grain are known. Again, maize grains are well anchored to the cob axis, as is evident when eating corn on the cob. More curiously perhaps, the corn ear is covered by numerous leaf bases (the husks), and this together with the firm anchorage effectively precludes seed dispersal, without human intervention. Finally, maize is reduced virtually to a single culm, in contrast to the numerous tillers we might expect in a wild grass.

Maize is so changed during domestication that the matter of its wild ancestor remains open. No wild grass currently known provides the obvious progenitor of cultivated maize. One option is to seek among maize breeders' collections for mutants that would be more characteristic of wild grasses, such as 'pod' corn, multi-tillering and inflorescences containing both female and male spikelets. By bringing such mutants together, could we reverse maize evolution and recreate a possible approximation, a living plant, that taught us something of maize ancestry? For further details of this fascinating approach, see the clássic study by Mangelsdorf et al. (1964).

## Non-cereal grasses in cultivation

It is evident that forage grasses provide a major feedstuff for animals and such grasses vary from one environment to another. In the temperate regions *Lolium perenne* is important together with other ingredients of permanent pasture such as species of *Festuca, Cynosurus cristatus, Dactylis glomerata, Phleum pratense* and various species of *Poa*. Forage grasses in the tropics include dozens of examples reflecting that grass species in general are more numerous there. Important forage grasses include many genera, for example *Andropogon, Anthephora, Brachiaria, Cenchrus, Chloris, Digitaria, Eragrostis, Lasiurus, Panicum, Paspalum, Pennisetum, Saccharum,* and many others.

Apart from forage, some grasses are cultivated for other purposes. *Cymbopogon citratus* (lemon grass) has aromatic leaves that find a place in flavouring foods. *Coix lachryma-jobi* apart from being a minor cereal has a hard shelled variety that provides ornamental beads. Some grasses have medical claims made for them which, perhaps, deserve to be regarded with some circumspection.

Two grasses important in land stabilisation are *Ammophila arenaria* (marram grass) which fixes sand dunes and, increasingly of consequence, *Vetiveria zizanioides* used to create terraced hillsides in the moist tropics. This latter has long been grown for its aromatic roots, the source of vetiver oil.

The grasses mentioned in this chapter are either those that are planted deliberately or those which, if they self-perpetuate, are welcome or acceptable. Less welcome species are referred to as 'weeds' and to these we now turn.

# Chapter 9

# Grasses as Weedy Colonists

In Chapter 1 attention was drawn to the role of grasses in colonising disturbed habitats, an idea that will now be explored more fully.

At tropical latitudes it is possible to draw a transect across a group of environments from rainforest through monsoon forest to thorn woodland, savanna and finally desert. Along such a transect trees (and the epiphytes they support) become less and less conspicuous ingredients in the flora as available moisture diminishes. Grasses, by contrast, become more and more evident reaching their most impressive appearance in the savanna where they comprise the dominant ingredient. As one continues along the transect to the desert, vegetation almost disappears. Even here grasses retain a tenacious hold as thinly scattered clumps. It is helpful to recognise that if the savanna desertifies it leaves behind a remnant grass flora. If, however, the situation changes and the desert begins to retreat grasses are among the first plants to exploit the changed circumstances that permit the colonisation of open ground.

Open habitats today are commonplace. They include roadworks, and building sites often on an immense scale together with episodes of forest clearance. To these disturbances attributable to human beings one can add other more natural instances of coastal and riverine erosion and accumulation, wind blown surface matter, volcanic lava flows and deposition as moraines from melted glacier snouts. All these open habitats present grasses with no new problems but rather the opportunities for colonisation to which their biology is so superbly adapted.

## Cultivation

Against the background just described cultivation has a new perspective. Ploughing, harrowing and sowing produce a systematic disturbance of an immense area of the world's land surface once or, in favoured locations, two or three times a year. Such activity prevents the establishment of a tree cover and retains an environment that some grasses can readily exploit. Such habitats are not merely open, they are often provided with water and fertiliser.

An interesting fact and one that contributes to our understanding is that with the removal of (say) a wheat or barley harvest so few volunteer seedlings will survive land preparation into the next crop. To establish a new crop will require a significant input of seed while weed populations will survive and provide competition indefinitely. Since cultivation allows weeds to survive unaided whereas seed of the new crop must be added each season a cynic might conclude that agriculture was more suited to weeds than crops.

**Crops and weed control**

Although cereals are annuals and grass weeds can be either annuals or perennials disturbed ground favours each of them. The farmer's problem therefore is to shift the balance of advantage toward the crop. To achieve this, three contrasted approaches have emerged to replace the laborious and time consuming hand weeding. These are as follows.

*1) Minimal cultivation.* Here after removing the previous crop only a narrow line of soil is disturbed to plant the new seed (with the added advantage of requiring less fuel). In practice, cereals grown on such minimally disturbed soil are less productive and the method has not been widely adopted.

*2) Herbicides.* An alternative approach is the use of chemicals which kill weeds selectively leaving the crop unharmed. Such a technique is attractive to a research-based company (which may in addition seek to increase resistance to the herbicide in the crop plant by breeding). Given the increasing influence of environmentalists nowadays the cost of developing 'satisfactory' chemicals seems likely increasingly to become prohibitive.

*3) Biological control.* Breeders have long recognised that a plant altered genetically might be made resistant to some disease or pest. The same reasoning could lead to the identification of more virulent diseases or pests that would selectively attack pernicious weeds. Such artificially contrived agents should target a weed while leaving crops unharmed.

Weeds, by their nature, are robust plants and able competitors. While therefore, in theory, selectively damaging agents might be found, in practice, the demands on the investigator are severe. Moreover what is called a weed under some circumstances might be viewed elsewhere more favourably. *Imperata cylindrica* seen sometimes as a noxious weed can also provide both thatch and rough grazing. Even if a suitably damaging agent were found one should consider most carefully the well nigh irrevocable consequence of introducing it.

It will be clear from the foregoing summary that weeds will remain a feature of agriculture indefinitely and it is now appropriate, therefore, to consider the weeds themselves more closely.

## Major grass weeds

An instructive comparison is as follows. Kasasian (1964) listed for the small island of Trinidad 20 significant grass weed species. Later (1971) the same author discussing weed control in the tropics listed half this number of which most, though not all, occurred on the Trinidad list. It is thus possible to distinguish weeds of local interest from those that range far more widely and which are therefore of greater concern.

A more recent treatment (Holm et al., 1977) lists 18 grass weeds of major importance and 22 of more secondary significance. When compared with other plant families it is evident that the Poaceae is a major source of agricultural weeds. Given that the Poaceae provides all our cereals requiring the habitats that grasses do can we be in any way surprised that so many of our weeds are grasses?

Rather than merely list grass weeds, Table 9.1 sets them out by taxonomic affinity from which a number of observations can be made. These are that the five major subfamilies have each contributed weeds though not to the same extent. Conspicuously, the Panicoideae is a source of weeds though with an evident concentration in the subtribe Setariinae. However, those species deemed especially important (in bold type) are relatively scattered. Of the 10 most important grasses only *Avena fatua* is $C_3$. Of all 32 grasses listed only five are $C_3$ a reflection of the greater diversity of grasses found at lower latitudes.

An agriculturalist from the temperate region could well protest that he did not have to deal only with the grass species shown in the table and could mention *Alopecurus myosuroides* (blackgrass), *Elytrigia (Agropyron) repens* (twitch or couch grass), *Poa annua* (annual poa grass) among many others quite apart from numerous dicotyledons. Here we return to the point that some weeds have a more local significance. That said, the situation need not remain static. *Imperata cylindrica* once confined to Africa is now a major grass weed throughout the tropics. *Echinochloa crus-galli* of Asian origin is today a generalised tropical weed. Stace (1991) records that *Digitaria sanguinalis* now occurs in the British Isles. Given increasing contact between agricultural regions of the world the number of significant weed species with which we must deal will inevitably increase. For a recent text on tropical grassy weeds see Baker and Terry (1991).

## Rice weeds

Rice paddy is an unusual habitat and one therefore instructive when considering the weeds that occur there. It is possible that culture by flooding (submergence) and rice transplanting were two early means of combating weed competition. Even so, a range of rice weeds flourish in paddy conditions, for example *Oryza sativa* (red rice).

More surprisingly, persistent rice weeds include, from Table 9.1, *Cynodon dactylon, Digitaria sanguinalis, Echinochloa colona, E. crus-galli, Eleusine in-*

Table 9.1. Taxonomic affinities of weedy grasses (species in bold type are major weeds).

| Subfamily | Tribe | Subtribe | A = annual   P = perennial<br>Genera & species |
|-----------|-------|----------|-------------------------------------------------|
| Arundinoideae | Arundineae | - | *Phragmites australis* P<br>*P. karka* P |
| Bambusoideae | Oryzeae | - | *Leersia hexandra* P |
| Chloridoideae | Cynodonteae<br>Eragrostideae | Chloridinae<br>Eleusininae | **Cynodon dactylon** P<br>*Dactyloctenium aegyptium* A<br>**Eleusine indica** A<br>*Leptochloa chinensis* A<br>*L. panicea* A |
| Panicoideae | Paniceae | Cenchrinae | *Cenchrus echinatus* A<br>*Pennisetum clandestinum* P<br>*P. pedicellatum* P<br>*P. polystachion* P<br>*P. purpureum* P |
| | | Digitariinae | *Digitaria abysinnica* P<br>*D. ciliaris* A<br>**D. sanguinalis** A |
| | | Ischaeminae | *Ischaemum rugosum* A |
| | | Rottboelliinae | **Rottboellia cochinchinensis** A |
| | | Saccharinae | **Imperata cylindrica** P |
| | | Setariinae | *Axonopus compressus* P<br>*Brachiaria mutica* P<br>**Echinochloa colona** A<br>**E. crus-galli** A<br>*Panicum maximum* P<br>*P. repens* P<br>**Paspalum conjugatum** P<br>*P. dilatum* P<br>*Setaria verticillata* A<br>*S. viridis* A |
| | | Sorghinae | *Sorghum halepense* P |
| Pooideae | Aveneae<br>Poeae | Aveninae<br>- | **Avena fatua** A<br>*Lolium temulentum* A |

*dica* and *Sorghum halepense*. That one might first associate these with dryland agriculture and that, additionally, they frequent rice paddy underlines something of the range of their adaptability. For an extended discussion of rice weeds see Moody (1991).

## Some Weeds Re-assessed Sociologically

While we may sympathise with the irritation or dismay a farmer might feel for a weedy field, as biologists a more judicious view is appropriate. *Imperata cylindrica* is described as 'aggressively rhizomatous' and clearly difficult to eradicate as a result. Such a growth habit is however an asset in allowing *Imperata* to resist soil erosion under intense and prolonged rainfall as does *Pennisetum clandestinum*. *I. cylindra rubra*, a striking red stemmed variant, is now sold as an ornamental for temperate gardens and described as 'rare', 'choice' and 'impressive'. A comparable instance is *Cynodon dactylon,* an immensely successful grass throughout the tropics. At low latitudes as an ingredient in pasture it is regarded as a sign of degeneration that could (and should) be replaced with *Brachiaria decumbens* or *Andropogon gayanus* or some other more productive grass. And yet so sought after is *Cynodon dactylon* for an amenity grass that home owners will pay for cuttings of it to be laboriously hand planted to make large lawns. *Panicum maximum* is described as a weed. Even so many people of small means around the tropics tether their goats in roadside patches of this grass whose value is so widely recognised.

It is possible to recognise a paradox. To open up some habitat by forest clearance and ploughing makes possible (say) a cereal agriculture. If the farming is inadequate to the situation and the land has to be abandoned through severe weed growth this is the first step toward eventual re-establishment of the forest cover. Here the value of the weed cover is restorative and was a recognisable stage of a less settled form of agriculture when the cultivator moved on to a new location.

## Some Weeds Re-assessed Genetically

Earlier in this chapter attention was drawn to the problems of biological control of weed species. Clearly, the closer the genetic relationship between a weed and the crop it infests the greater the difficulty of finding an agent that will confine itself to the weed.

Closeness of relationship between a crop and its companion weeds is a topic with many facets. Cultivated *Sorghum* will cross naturally with wild *S. verticilliflorum*. Fertile hybrids result producing spikelets that shatter as do those of a wild grass. It is known in the Near East that newly introduced tetraploid wheats can eventually provide the means, sometimes, of genetic change in wild tetraploid wheats growing nearby. Again, *Avena fatua* can be changed genetically by its association as a weed in new oat varieties. Given this closeness of relationship the prospects for biological control of the weed whilst not damaging the crop seem well nigh impossible. The matter, however, can be regarded differently.

Before the dawn of agriculture clearly no distinction could be made between crop and weed. Only when certain grasses, for whatever reason, were preferred could others be regarded with disfavour. If, however, genetic exchange were possible then the vigour that allows weeds to survive unaided could perhaps in some measure be transferred to the emerging cultivated plant. Again if that vigour were in part disease or- pest resistance the idea arises that companion weed races provided genetic support for their associated crops. Harlan (1965) took this view even further:

> "We may summarise, then, by stating our conclusion that the weed races have played an immensely important role in the evolution of cultivated plants. They have served as reservoirs of reserve germplasm, periodically injecting portions of it into the crops under conditions that would most favour increases in variability, heterozygosity and heterosis. It is indeed possible to argue that some of our cultivated plants would never have succeeded as domesticates without the genetic support of their companion weed races."

Assuming Harlan's viewpoint to be true what happens if a crop is transported beyond the ecological range of its companion weed races? Obviously, the crop would be genetically isolated unless, as in breeding programmes, related wild species are incorporated into the crossing programme. On this basis modern breeding is merely a systematised extension of what has in nature been happening over several thousand years.

While such a view reassesses weeds genetically we must recognise that in any given situation most weeds will be unrelated to that particular crop and the problems of competition that diminish yields remain a day to day preoccupation for the farmer.

# A Critical Glossary of the Grasses

The treatment here is to interest as much as to define. Some terms, even those long in use, yield thought-provoking ambiguities when carefully reconsidered.

Are botanical terms descriptive or analytic? They can be either. A leaf with a surface bloom can be described as glaucous and that is uncontroversial. If a leaf belonging to a grass is referred to as a 'phyllode', what seemed to be leaf is now regarded as an expanded petiole. The approach is 'analytic'. The matter does not rest there since this view advocated by Arber (1918) is unhesitatingly rejected by Tomlinson (1970). Similarly, by opting for a 'pooid' or 'panicoid' interpretation of a rice spikelet, 'glume' and 'lemma' are terms that can be applied by different botanists to the same structure.

Again, some terms are more or less exclusive to grasses or have been extended from them subsequently. These include 'culm' and 'tiller' and seem to bear the stamp of practicality. Next there are those seemingly botanical, but used for grasses in a way that properly surprises other botanists. They, assuming a pedicel supports a floret, find in grasses that it supports a spikelet. Moreover, what is a grass inflorescence? Do we mean the panicle or its component spikelets or both and are what we call 'racemes' condensed panicles? Reassuringly, some botanical terms are used for grasses no differently than elsewhere.

The approach adopted here is discursive where necessary. Etymology, surprisingly, is of relatively little use. While it tells us what a word means, that is of little help when we want to know how it is used.

*Abaxial/Adaxial:* Strictly, this refers to whether the surface faces away from or toward the axis of the originating primordium, i.e. outer or inner face. Commonly used for the lower and upper leaf surfaces respectively, but may also be applied to (say) lemma, palea or glumes. A vertical structure therefore has abaxial and adaxial surfaces.

*Adventitious:* Applied to roots arising from stem nodes to distinguish from those originating at or from the primary root emerging from the germinating seed. cf. *Seminal*

*Agamospermy:* see *Apomixis.*

*Aleurone:* One or more layers of cells formed from the outermost cells of the endosperm which store substantial quantities of protein. cf. *Bran, Grist*

*Andromonoecious:* Hermaphrodite and male flowers on the same inflorescence, as in many panicoid grasses.

*Anemophily:* Wind-mediated pollination.

*Annual:* Completing the life cycle within a year. cf. *Ephemeral, Perennial*

*Anthesis:* Pollen dehiscence due to opening of the anthers. In functionally cleistogamous plants it precedes any flower opening. cf. *Cleistogamy, Protandry, Protogyny*

*Antipodal:* Applies to nuclei and/or cells near the chalaza within the embryo sac. In grasses their number and the amount of DNA per nucleus are variable. cf. *Egg apparatus*

*Apomixis:* Commonly used now to describe non-sexual reproduction via the seed. cf. *Apospory, Diplospory, Pseudogamy.* (The literature is not consistent: formerly apomixis meant all forms of vegetative reproduction including tillers, rhizomes etc. The term 'agamospermy' was used for vegetative reproduction via the seed as a form of apomixis.)

*Apospory:* Accounts in grasses for most species where apomixis occurs, and is the development of an unreduced embryo sac from a somatic cell of the ovule in the nucellus, but can occur in the integuments. cf. *Apomixis, Diplospory, Pseudogamy*

*Arm cell:* Specialised leaf cells, characteristic of Bambuseae and typically 'm'-shaped. cf. *Fusoid cell*

*Auricle:* Extensions to the leaf lamina projecting toward and sometimes enclosing the stem. Well known in wheat. cf. *Oral setae*

*Awn:* A stiff projection usually from the lemma or glume either from the tip or the abaxial surface. If 'knee-shaped' the awn is 'geniculate'.

*Baccate fruit:* The pericarp (the caryopsis wall) is fleshy in some bamboos such as *Melocanna.*

*Bagasse:* The residue of sugar cane stem after rollers have expressed the juice.

*Boot:* The flag leaf as it encloses the inflorescences before ear emergence. cf. *Flag leaf*

*Bract/Bracteole:* A (sometimes leaf-like) structure subtending an inflorescence while a bracteole or bractlet subtends a flower. Since the spikelet in its various forms and the inflorescence branching system seems to have been repeatedly 'condensed' the bract or bracteole status of glumes, lemma and palea is dubious.

*Braird:* A stand of newly emerged seedlings.

*Bran:* Husk of grain separated from the flour after grinding. In wheat, bran includes pericarp, integuments and nucellus derivatives. cf. *Aleurone, Grist*

*Branch:* An axillary bud developing either from the primary stem or one of its subsidiaries obviously above the ground. cf. *Rhizome, Stolon, Tiller*

*Branch complement:* An axillary bud can, especially in bamboos, divide to produce subsidiary apices, a group of which develops to produce the characteristic cluster. cf. *Gremial*

*Bulb/Bulbil:* 'Bulbous' shaped structures occur in Poaceae, but true bulbs, formed from swollen leaf bases, can be confused with corms. *Melica bulbosa* is corm forming, for example. Ref. Burns (1946). cf. *Corm*

*Bulliform cell:* Bubble shaped cells occurring in groups between leaf veins, poor in contents but water-retentive. Alterations in their shape caused by loss of water allows leaves to inroll into a more tubular shape, thus diminishing transpiration.

*$C_3$ grasses:* Those species (commonly temperate) whose first detectable photosynthetic intermediate sugar precursor is the 3-carbon compound 3-phosphoglycerate.

*$C_4$ grasses:* Those species (commonly tropical) whose first detectable photosynthetic intermediate sugar precursor is a 4-carbon compound, either malate

or aspartate. See Chapter 6.

*$^{13}$C:* This isotope of carbon is of interest in photosynthesis because $C_3$ plants discriminate against $^{13}CO_2$ relative to $^{12}CO_2$, more than do $C_4$ plants. See Chapter 6.

*Caespitose:* Tufted.

*Carpel:* Ovule-bearing structure that either singly or with others provides ovary, style and stigma tissue (collectively the pistil). In grasses the remnants of three, or more commonly two, carpels are believed to form the ovary and 'share' a common ovule.

*Caryopsis:* The grass fruit, normally dry at maturity, consisting of a single seed within, and including the ovary. cf. *Baccate fruit, Pericarp*

*Centrifugal/Centripetal:* Applied to chloroplasts in bundle sheath cells, which are concentrated away from or toward the xylem cells respectively. See Chapter 6.

*Chalaza:* Area of the ovule at the opposite end to the micropyle.

*Chasmogamy:* Refers to a flower which opens so as to permit both cross- and self-pollination. cf. *Anthesis, Cleistogamy*

*Chorology:* The study of distribution and composition of elements in a flora (or fauna).

*Cleistogamy:* Refers to a flower which remains closed to permit only self-pollination (and by implication, self-fertilisation) although sometimes the flower opens later, as in wheat. cf. *Anthesis, Chasmogamy*

*Cleistogene:* Modified spikelets containing self-compatible flowers within basal leaf sheaths.

*Coleoptile:* A sheath of tissue enclosing the shoot and from which leaves and the stem subsequently emerge. cf. *Coleorhiza, Plumule*

*Coleorhiza:* A sheath of tissue enclosing the radicle prior to emergence. In monocots, the radicle is somewhat short lived, the bulk of roots (adventitious) developing from the stem nodes.

*Collar:* Structure at the base of the ear which marks the transition from stem to rachis; a rudimentary leaf. See 'Photorespiration' in Chapter 6, p. 61.

*Conduplicate:* Two parts folded together lengthwise as in emerging leaves of *Poa.* cf. *Involute*

*Connective:* The band of tissue linking each anther, to which the distal tip of the filament is attached.

*Corm:* Enlarged, swollen stem tissue as in *Arrhenatherum elatius. Poa* curiously has both bulb-forming and corm-forming species, respectively *P. bulbosa* and *P. nodosa.* See Burns, (1946). cf. *Bulb/Bulbil*

*Corn:* A general name for barley, oats, rye and wheat in Britain. In America, corn refers to maize and the four crops mentioned earlier are referred to as 'small grains'.

*Culm:* Aerial stems of grasses. Normally vertical but can be prostrate or spreading. cf. *Tiller, Uniculm*

*Culm sheath:* A leaf sheath wrapped around the culm with a diminutive leaf lamina, as shown by bamboos.

*Decarboxylating enzymes:* NAD-ME, nicotinamide adenine dinucleotide-malate enzyme; NADP-ME, nicotinamide adenine dinucleotide phosphate-malate enzyme; PEP/CK (or PCK) phosphenol pyruvate carboxykinase. These are the alternative enzymes which release $CO_2$ from $C_4$ acids in the bundle sheath cells of species with $C_4$ photosynthesis.

*Diaphragm:* The sheet of tissue (woody in bamboos) separating the lumen of each internode in hollow stemmed grasses.

*Diaspore:* Unit of dispersal. In cultivated wheat and maize the naked grain is separated from all the surrounding scales. In barley, oats and many other species, the palea and lemma are normally abscised with the grain (apart from naked grain types). In *Tristachya* and wild *Hordeum* spp., groups of three spikelets are shed. Numerous other variants occur.

*Dichogamous:* Male and female organs mature at different times permitting cross-pollination. cf. *Protandry, Protogyny*

*Dioecy:* Male and female flowers borne on separate plants. cf. *Monoecy*

*Diplospory:* An embryo sac developed from an unreduced megaspore mother cell. In grasses this is relatively rare but is reported in *Poa, Calamagrostis, Eragrostis* and *Triticum.* cf. *Apomixis, Apospory, Pseudogamy*

*Disjunct:* One genus (or species) whose representatives are at separate locations. It does not follow automatically but it can be inferred that their distribution was once continuous.

*Distichous:* Parts arranged in two rows one each on opposite sides as in grass leaves and the florets within a spikelet. (Members of Cyperaceae have parts in threes thus providing a simple contrast with Poaceae). cf. *Trimerous*

*Ear:* A general term for a cereal inflorescence which is compact or a spike. In maize the male inflorescence is a tassel. The female is an ear from which protrude the stigmas described as 'silks'. Seeds removed from the maize ear expose the axis called a 'cob'.

*Egg apparatus:* The association of egg cell with two synergids (in Poaceae) at the micropyle end of the embryo sac.

*Elaiosome:* Oil bearing appendages sought by insects and facilitating seed dispersal. Occurs in several grasses including *Yakirra.*

*Embellum:* see *Ovule appendage.*

*Embryo sac:* Within the ovule, the haploid megaspore (resulting from meiosis) undergoes three further sets of divisions to produce eight nuclei. These are rearranged as the egg apparatus, polar nuclei and antipodals. The embryo sac is the megagametophyte of flowering plants.

*Endemic:* Confined to a particular area. *Yakirra,* for example, is endemic to Australia. Endemism occurs in grasses but is not as important as in the palms, for example.

*Endosperm:* Tissue originating at double fertilisation from union of two polar nuclei with one male gamete. Flowering plants are unique in that the male parental genome contributes to the nutrient tissue for its offspring.

*Ephemeral:* Very short-lived: a plant completing its life cycle in appreciably less than twelve months. cf. *Annual, Perennial*

*Epiblast:* A projection from the embryonic shoot opposite the scutellum. If monocots are assumed to be derived from dicots, the epiblast can be interpreted as a vestigial second cotyledon. Alternatively, the epiblast can be interpreted as a projection of the (stem encircling) attachment of the single cotyledon, the scutellum. The epiblast is small in *Avena* and *Triticum* and larger in *Stipa* and *Oryza,* for example.

*Extravaginal:* A branch which penetrates the base of its subtending leaf. cf. *Intravaginal.* The genera *Thyridolepis* and *Neurachne,* supposedly closely related members of the Neurachninae, differ in this character.

*Flag leaf:* The last (and subtending) leaf before inflorescence emergence. As the largest and best illuminated leaf, its photosynthetic capacity can appreciably influence yield. If the sheath is enlarged and partially encloses the inflorescence, it is referred to as a spatheole.

*Fusoid cell:* Large central cells in the leaves of Bambuseae, on either side of the vascular bundle and surrounded by 'arm cells'.

*Geniculate:* A 'knee-shaped' appearance normally found in awns emerging from the abaxial surface of the lemma as in *Arrhenatherum* or *Avena.*

*Glume:* Bracts at the base of a spikelet (usually two) which do not themselves contain florets and are thus 'sterile'. In bamboos several 'glumes' might be present, but these are of uncertain affinity. In *Oryza* , depending on the interpretation of the flower, one can regard both glumes as suppressed or locate identifiable glumes elsewhere.

*Gluten:* A protein in wheat flour that adds elasticity to dough. Genetically it was contributed to hexaploid (bread) wheat from *Triticum tauschii* (*Aegilops squarrosa*). It functions by allowing the bubbles of $CO_2$ produced by yeast to be retained, thus allowing the bread to rise (or be leavened).

*Gregarious flowering:* Applied commonly to bamboos when all individuals of a species flowers collectively after a long interval. 'Mast' flowering is the term preferred by Janzen (1976) but refers to the same phenomenon.

*Gremial:* Growing in a pollard-like cluster - applied to the branch complement.

*Grist:* A mixture of grain used for milling or malting. cf. *Bran*

*Heritability:* Refers to the extent to which a character can be inherited (more strictly: that proportion of the variability within a population which is due to heritable differences between individuals). Some characters are highly heritable such as those of spikelet morphology. Others, such as plant size, are more subject to environmental influences.

*Heterofertilisation:* An occurrence where the egg and central cells of one embryo sac are fertilised by male gametes originating in different pollen tubes.

*Hilum:* The scar on the seed surface revealed by abscission of the funicle (seed stalk).

*Holocarpic (Monocarpic):* Applied primarily to bamboos that die after flowering and fruiting but is also applicable to annual grasses or to the individual flowering culms of perennial species.

*Homology:* Used in two senses. It can mean corresponding chromosomes arising from each parent that will pair at meiosis. Applied to morphology, the lodicule of a grass corresponds to a petal of (say) *Tradescantia*, implying a common origin.

*Ideotype:* A man-made design for a plant, intended to aid a breeder in producing an improved variety. Although often presented as a diagram it does of course imply certain physiological properties such as high harvest index, more nutritional grains or improved pest and disease resistance. Classic refs: Donald (1968); Bunting (1971)

*Induration:* The indurated structure is one surrounded or enclosed by its supporting structure, as with spikelets within the rachis of *Oropetium*. Induration normally means hardening, but not invariably so in grasses. Owing possibly to the influence of genes from *Tripsacum,* the hard cob of maize is said to be indurated.

*Inflorescence:* A collection of spikelets arranged on a common branching system. cf. *Panicle, Raceme, Spike*

*Ingera (Enjora):* A fermented paste of flour subsequently cooked and often eaten with peppered meat. An Ethiopian food prepared from t'ef (*Eragrostis tef* ).

*Integument:* Layers of cells surrounding the ovule. Grass ovules are invested by two layers of tissue and are therefore bitegmic. In both Panicoids and Pooids the inner integument covers the ovule sufficiently completely to form the micropyle, whilst the outer integument is respectively less and more complete in covering the ovule. cf. *Bran*

*Internode:* The interval on a stem rhizome or rachis between two nodes; typically conspicuous in grasses. cf. *Phytomer*

*Intravaginal:* A branch which remains enclosed by its subtending leaf for a substantial period of development. cf. *Extravaginal*

*Involucre:* In general botanical usage a whorl of small leaves or bracts standing close underneath a flower or flowers. In *Cenchrus* the involucre is formed from sterile branches.

*Involute:* Inrolled to include the adaxial surface. cf. *Revolute*

*Iterauctant:* (Lat. *iteratus* - repeated) A term applied to a congested bamboo inflorescence where pseudospikelets occur producing successive orders of branching. cf. *Pseudospikelet, Semelauctant*

*Keeled:* Ridged like the bottom of a boat. In grasses the ridges of the palea are of interest since two rather than one can be detected.

*Kranz and non-Kranz:* Refer respectively to whether the vascular bundles of transverse leaf sections possess photosynthetic bundle sheaths, indicating C₄ or C₃ types respectively. See Chapter 6.

*Lamina:* The extended flattened portion of the leaf as opposed to the sheath enclosing the stem.

*Lemma:* The outer bract (?) / bracteole (?) which, together with the palea, encloses the flower. Of interest in its detailed variation and therefore taxonomic usefulness. In vestigial florets it is often the last structural remnant.

*Leptomorph:* See *Monopodial*

*Ligule:* The adaxial extension of leaf sheath at its junction with the lamina. An 'outer' ligule described for *Arundinaria* is simply an outer rim of the normal ligule.

*Lodicule:* The likely equivalent in grasses of the 'petal' seen elsewhere. Typically three in bamboos, two elsewhere. Lodicules inflate at anthesis to separate palea and lemma thus opening the floret.

*Macrohairs:* Large hairs found on grass leaf and stem surfaces but cf. *Microhairs.*

*Meristem:* A cluster of dividing cells comprising the root and stem apices. An intercalary meristem occurs at the base of grass leaves rendering them less damaged by animal grazing or lawn mowing.

*Mesocotyl:* An interpolated node in the grass seedling separating sheath and cotyledon.

*Mestome-sheath:* A sheath of tissue which, if present, directly surrounds the vascular bundle of a grass leaf. Such a leaf is coded XyMS+. If absent the leaf is coded XyMS-. In some cases, e.g. *Neurachne*, it is the inner layer of a double bundle sheath which is photosynthetic. Since a non-photosynthetic layer is then **not** interposed between the photosynthesising layer and the xylem, this grass type, though having double-sheathed bundles, is referred to as XyMS- (Hattersley and Watson, 1992). See Chapter 6.

*Metaxenia:* The phenomenon whereby tissues **outside** the embryo sac are influenced by the pollen source. This is known for date palm (*Phoenix*) and should not be confused with xenia, a situation known in *Zea*. cf. *Xenia*

*Microhairs:* Small hairs conveniently seen on leaf surfaces, which are of characteristic shapes for different groups of grasses. For detail see Watson and Dallwitz (1988), and Chapman (1992a). cf. *Macrohairs*

*Micropyle:* The aperture formed where the integuments do not completely envelop the nucellus. Before fertilisation it provides a port of entry for the pollen tube, and at seed germination ingress for moisture.

*Monoecy:* Separate male and female inflorescences on the same plant - maize is the most familiar example. cf. *Dioecy* (See Jones, 1934, where a simple genetic manipulation converts moneocy to dioecy.)

*Monopodial:* Rhizomes which run indefinitely, producing culms from lateral buds. The synonym 'leptomorph' seems superfluous. cf. *Sympodial*

*M.S.:* See *Mestome-sheath*

*Neck:* Constricted part at the base of segmented vegetative axes.

*Nerve:* Often used as a synonym for vein (or longitudinal vascular bundle). The animal associations are never appropriate when applied to plants. *Vein* is to be preferred.

*Nobilisation:* A process so far known only in *Saccharum* where *S. officinarum* x *S. spontaneum* provides a hybrid with an unreduced chromosome number from the female parent. See Bremer (1961).

*Node:* The junction between two internodes, conspicuous in grasses, from which leaves, adventitious roots and branches can arise. The successive changes in development of nodes along a stem is of interest. cf. *Phytomer.*

*Nucellus:* Ovule tissue internal to the integuments and surrounding the embryo sac. Normally transitory in seed development, one reference shows it massively enlarged in sorghum following *in vitro* pollination with maize (Dhaliwal and King, 1978).

*Operculum:* The 'lid' covering the single germ pore of a grass pollen grain. Ref. Heslop-Harrison (1961).

*Oral setae:* Conspicuous bristles at the junction of sheath and leaf. cf. *Auricle.*

*Ovule appendage:* In some genera, for example *Cenchrus* and *Pennisetum,* nucellar cells protrude through the micropyle providing a rim or even short tube whose function is unknown. Sometimes termed an 'embellum'.

*Panicle:* A branching inflorescence which in many genera is lax but in some instances is tightly compacted. *Eragrostis tef* shows this range within one species. cf. *Raceme, Spike.*

*Pedicel/Pedicellate spikelet*: A stalk supporting one of the paired spikelets found in andropogonoid grasses. Curiously, in other plant families the pedicel supports the flower arising on a peduncle.

*Perennial:* Surviving over several (or even many) seasons. Perhaps in extreme cases up to 6000 years (in *Phragmites australis*). Ref. Chapman (1990). cf. *Annual, Ephemeral*

*Pericarp:* Nominally the carpel tissue comprised of epi-, meso- and endo-carp that surrounds (in grasses) the single ovule. cf. *Baccate fruit, Testa*

*Petiole:* The leaf stalk. See the opening discussion of this Glossary.

*Phenetic:* Describing the appearance rather than the genetic constitution of an organism.

*Photorespiration:* Detectable in $C_3$ grasses where ribulose bisphosphate decarboxylase combines with oxygen rather than $CO_2$, eventually forming glycolate which is removed by a respiratory process. See Chapter 6.

*Photosynthesis:* The fixation of carbon as sugar from $CO_2$ and water with oxygen resulting. See Chapter 6.

*Phytomer:* A unit of development, defined as a leaf, the subadjacent internode, the node and its lateral bud, with adventitious roots if present. Ref. Clark and Fisher (1987). cf. *Node*

*Plicate:* Folded as a fan or approaching this condition.

*Plumule:* The embryonic shoot enclosed within, and later as it emerges from, the seed. cf. *Coleoptile*

*Polycross:* Random mating between members of a group of selected genotypes by allowing open pollination among them.

*Polygamy:* Refers to one plant having many sexual partners but the preferred term is panmixis or panmixia.

*Polyphyletic:* An individual taxon to which different (by implication very different) ancestors have contributed. cf. *Taxon*

*Proliferous:* The preferred alternative to *vivipary* (*q.v.*); it is applied to an inflorescence which has become vegetative.

*Prophyllum/Prophyll:* Perhaps the most ambiguous term in agrostology. Jackson (1928) regards it as equivalent to a palea. McClure (1966) on p.93 calls it the first foliar appendage subtending a pseudospikelet but on p. 312 (glossary) defines it as a sheathing organ found in vegetative and inflorescence branches. Clayton and Renvoize (1986) equate the palea with a diminished prophyll of an axillary branch. It is also used sometimes in reference to unexpanded tiller buds. Attempted classification: Forewarned of its ambiguity, the reader should ask him or herself if it is being used 'analytically' or 'descriptively'. In the former case are there, for example, implicit assumptions about phylogeny and 'branch condensations'? If the term is used only descriptively it is supposedly 'neutral' and what that author calls a prophyll carries no implication. It is to be hoped that the term will fall into disuse or that authors will (if they must use it) carefully define and consistently apply it. Turpin (1819) apparently coined the term setting up what Tomlinson (1970) called a 'wild goose chase'. Blaser (1944) after critical scrutiny regards the prophyllum as neither more nor less than a leaf, albeit sometimes modified.

*Protandry:* pollen shedding (anthesis) ahead of stigma receptivity. Conspicuous in many grasses.

*Protogyny:* Stigmas of a flower receptive ahead of pollen shedding (anthesis). Conspicuous in pearl millet. cf. *Dichogamous*

*Pseudogamy:* A variant of double fertilisation where one male gamete fuses with the central cell and one male gamete approaches but does not fertilise the egg. A contributory factor in some apomicts. cf. *Apomixis.*

*Pseudospikelet:* A structure found in some bamboos. If the inflorescence is indeterminate each rachis branch ends in a spikelet but at its base is a short rachis clothed with lemma-like bracts and containing a meristem that will develop and end in a spikelet. The whole process can be repeated as for example in *Bambusa multiplex*. Ref. McClure (1966). Clayton (1990) drew attention to the multibranched stem of bamboo in relation to the bamboo branching panicle and regards the pseudospikelet as of doubtful use as a descriptive term. cf. *Iterauctant, Semelauctant*

*Pulvinus:* A swollen joint caused either by moisture accumulation or differential growth. More common in tropical grasses.

*Raceme:* If a raceme is defined as an unbranched inflorescence on which flowers are borne on pedicels and the power of apical growth is retained, then the determinate inflorescences of grasses are not racemes. If apical growth is removed from the definition, 'raceme' might usefully be applied to grass spikate inflorescences. In reality, raceme is misleading since most spikate examples are probably supercompacted panicles. It is probably more accurate to regard all grass inflorescences as panicles that are either lax or showing varying degrees of condensation, thus appearing compact. cf. *Panicle, Pedicel*

*Rachilla/Rhachilla:* Subdivisions or branchlets of the rachis that support individual flowers, within the spikelet. cf. *Pedicel, Rachis*

*Rachis/Rhachis:* The structure forming the axis or axes of the inflorescence. In cultivated cereals the structure is 'non-shattering'. cf. *Rachilla*

*Ramassage:* The harvesting of wild grasses.

*Revolute:* Inrolled to include the abaxial surface. cf. *Involute*

*Rhizanthogenes:* Highly modified spikelets on underground stems (rhizomes). For example, *Eremitis.* cf. *Cleistogene*

*Rhizome:* Stems developing below ground and bearing scale leaves from whose axillary buds ascending stems can arise sympodially or monopodially. cf. *Branch, Stolon, Tiller*

*Root:* In grasses, as in most monocots, the

primary root system (sometimes called 'seminal' i.e. originating from the seed), is relatively short lived being replaced by adventitious roots arising from leaf bases.

*Rostrum*: A cylindrical thickening of the lemma below the base of the awn found in some American *Stipa* for example. cf. *Stipe*

*Savanna:* Grassland developing in semi-arid regions of the tropics and sub tropics.

*Scale leaf:* A dry rudimentary or diminished version of larger greener leaves seen elsewhere on the same plant.

*Scandent:* Climbing, without the aid of tendrils or, according to Jackson (1928), climbing in whatever manner.

*Sclerenchyma:* Lignified cells without protoplasts at maturity.

*Sclerenchymatous girder:* In cross-section an I-shaped structure comprised of a vascular bundle with sclerenchymatous cells toward the adaxial and abaxial surfaces (leaf- strengthening tissue).

*Scutellum:* The single absorptive cotyledon, abutting the endosperm. This latter is evanescent in *Melocalamus* and *Dinochloa* and the scutellum is consequently enlarged.

*S - cleft:* Space separating scutellum from coleorhiza.

*Semelauctant:* A term applied to simple panicles where pseudospikelets do not congest the inflorescence. cf. *Iterauctant, Pseudospikelets*

*Seminal:* Arising from the seed. Commonly used for the seedling root system. cf. *Adventitious*

*Sessile:* Literally, 'seated', that is arranged upon a supporting structure without a detectable stalk.

*Sessile spikelet:* One of the pair normally found in andropogonoid grasses, or a spikelet directly attached to the rachis, as in *Lolium* or *Triticum*. cf. *Pedicel/Pedicellate spikelet*

*Sheath*: Normally applied to that part of the leaf enclosing the stem though seen impressively in the husks surrounding a maize ear.

*Silica body:* Silicon dioxide is laid down in appreciable amounts in many grass leaves, impeding section cutting for example, or offering some resistance to grazing. The crystals form characteristic shapes for groups of grasses.

*Silica cells:* Those in which silica is deposited and which subsequently cease to be metabolically active.

*Sinus:* The depression between two lobes or teeth. Applied for example to the lemma tip in relation to the position of the awn.

*Spatheole:* A leaf-life structure enclosing or at least subtending, a grass inflorescence. In cereals the term flag leaf is the commoner alternative. See Clayton and Renvoize (1986) p. 354.

*Spike:* An imprecise term applied to inflorescences with sessile spikelets, or sometimes to compact inflorescences. In no way comparable in importance to the term 'spikelet'. cf. *Panicle, Raceme*

*Spikelet:* The key reproductive structure in grasses where (usually) two glumes subtend a group of flowers. Variations in the spikelet form a principal part of grass taxonomy. cf. *Pseudospikelet*.

*Sterilisation* (within the spikelet): An 'evolutionary' concept whereby once functional flowers are thought to have become degenerate. 'Downward sterilisation' is an important characteristic of pooid grasses, whilst 'upward sterilisation' is found in panicoids. Where the spikelet is one flowered and has an indistinct arrangement of chaffy scales either process might have occurred, which some workers have claimed for the one-flowered rice spikelet.

*Stipe:* A stalk, but applied for example in *Microlaena stipoides* to that between the diminutive glumes and the florets. The genus *Stipa* apparently alludes to the stalked awns. cf. *Rostrum*

*Stolon:* Horizontal stems produced above ground, rooting at some nodes. cf. *Branch, Rhizome, Tiller*

*Sward:* A growth habit maintained by rhizomes or stolons where the shoots, perhaps grazed, form a layer over the ground. cf. *Tussock*

*Sympodial:* Applied to rhizomes where the apex turns upward to produce a culm. A superfluous synonym is 'pachymorph'. cf. *Monopodial*

*Synergids:* The two cells (in Poaceae) associated with the egg cell and collectively comprising the egg apparatus. One synergid is functional – the 'degenerating synergid' into which the pollen tube enters and discharges.

*Syphonogamy:* The delivery of gametes by a tube - in flowering plants the pollen tube which at its terminus enters the synergid to discharge.

*S Z:* The two-gene, multiple-allele incompatibility system, governing pollen-stigma interaction and apparently exclusive to the grasses. See Chapter 3.

*Tabashir:* Silica deposited within the culms of some bamboo species.

*Taxon:* A useful 'catchall' term that, depending on context, can refer to family, genus or species, i.e. a taxonomic group.

*Terete:* Circular in transverse section.

*Testa:* The matured outer layer of the seed, however it is derived. Normally it consists of the two ovule integuments, but in most grasses its close association with the pericarp complicates delineation. *Sporobolus* is interesting because the pericarp extrudes the seed.

*Tiller:* A subsidiary culm arising at or near the base of the primary culm or one of its earlier subsidiaries. The grass habit is more 'bunched' (caespitose) if the rhizome or stolon connecting the tiller to its origin is shorter. cf. *Branch, Rhizome, Stolon*

*Trimerous*: Arranged in threes. In grasses the floral parts show modifications of this, being more strongly trimerous in bamboos, less so elsewhere. cf. *Distichous*

*Tussock:* A growth habit where a collection of shoot apices forms a dome above the surrounding soil (or water as sometimes in the case of *Molinia*, for example). cf. *Sward*

*Uniculm:* A growth habit where the aerial part of the plant is confined to a single (fruit bearing) shoot.

*Utricle:* A modified leaf base found, for example, in *Coix*.

*Valvule:* A largely discarded term used to describe the palea. There is no case for its retention.

*Vegetative reproduction:* Nowadays used to include rhizomatous stoloniferous and tiller multiplication cf. *Apomixis.*

*Vein:* The visible strand running (usually) the length of a stem or leaf, representing a vascular bundle and associated strengthening tissues. cf. *Nerve*

*Vernalisation:* The process whereby prolonged cold treatment induces the formation of the reproductive primordia. Without it, a true winter cereal, sown in spring, would remain vegetative.

*Versatile:* Applied to anthers with connective pivots on the filament thereby assisting pollen shedding.

*Vivipary:* An absurd term meaning 'born alive' but this is true of any functional propagule. In practice it means a relatively differentiated propagule where stem, leaves and perhaps even roots are evident, especially if developed from what would have been an inflorescence. cf. *Proliferous* (the preferred term)

*Xenia:* Known and well documented in *Zea*, it refers to the ability of the pollen source to affect endosperm colour or flavour. cf. *Metaxenia*

*XyMS:* See *Mestome-sheath*

# Recommended Further Reading

Anon. (1984) *Forage and browse plants for arid and semi-arid Africa.* IBPGR/RBG, Kew, pp. 293.
> A compendium of grasses and legumes, giving botanical and ecological information on each species included, with comments on their agricultural usefulness.

Bonnett O. T. (1966) *Inflorescences of Maize, Wheat, Rye, Barley and Oats: their initiation and development.* University of Illinois College of Agriculture, Agriculture Experiment Station Bulletin 721.
> This is the classic treatment of reproductive ontogeny in these cereals. A better illustrated account, but more limited in species covered is Kirby and Appleyard (1984).

Chapman G. P. (ed.) (1992) *Desertified Grasslands: their Biology and Management.* Academic Press, London, pp. 360.

Dahlgren R. M. T., Clifford H. T. and Yeo P. F. (1985) *The Families of the Monocotyledons.* Springer Verlag, Heidelberg, pp. 520.
> A comprehensive text with numerous diagrams that provides an up-to-date view of relationships among monocotyledonous families.

Grosser D. and Liese W. (1971) On the anatomy of Asian bamboos, with special reference to their vascular bundles. *Wood Science and Technology* 5: 290-312.

Hitchcock A. S. and Chase A. (1950) *Manual of the Grasses of the United States.* Dover Publications Inc., New York. 2 vols.
> A comprehensive flora.

Hubbard C. E. (1984) *Grasses: a guide to their structure, identification, uses and distribution in the British Isles.* 3rd edition, Penguin Books Ltd., London, pp. 476.

Kirby E. J. M. and Appleyard M. (1984). *Cereal Development Guide.* 2nd edition. National Agricultural Centre, Arable Unit, Stoneleigh, pp. 95.

Lazzeri P.A., Kollmorgen J. and Lörz H. (1990) *In vitro* technology. In: Chapman G. P. (ed.) *Reproductive Versatility in the Grasses.* Cambridge University Press, pp. 182-219.
> This provides an up-to-date assessment and shows how far grasses are responsive to the newer genetic techniques.

Renvoize S. A. and Clayton W. D. (1992) Classification and evolution of the grasses. In: Chapman G. P. (ed.) *Grass Evolution and Domestication.* Cambridge University Press, pp. 3-37.
> This covers in detail the possible origin of the Bamboo pseudospikelet and the grass spikelet, and describes the major features of each of the subfamilies.

Söderstrom T. R., Hilu K. W., Campbell C. S. and Barkworth M. E. (eds) (1987) *Grass Systematics and Evolution.* Smithsonian Institute Press, Washington D. C., pp. 472.
> A comprehensive review of its subject by leading authorities.

Watson L. and Dallwitz M. J. (1992) *The Grass Genera of the World.* CAB International, Wallingford, pp. 1024.
> The printed compendium of information on all grass genera, originally available as a computer database.

# References

Arber A. (1918) The phyllode theory of the monocotyledonous leaf with special reference to anatomical evidence. *Annals of Botany* 32: 465-501.

Baker F. W. G. and Terry P. J. (eds) (1991) *Tropical Grassy Weeds.* CAB International, Wallingford, pp. 203.

Bentham G. and Hooker J. D. (1924) *Handbook of the British Flora.* L. Reeve & Co., Ashford, Kent, pp. 606.

Björkman O., Pearcy R. and Nobs M. (1971) Hybrids between *Atriplex* species with and without β-carboxylation photosynthesis. *Carnegie Inst. Washington Yearbook* 69: 640-648.

Blaser H. W. (1944) Studies in the morphology of Cyperaceae. II. The Prophyll. *American Journal of Botany* 31: 53-64.

Bremer G. (1961) Problems in breeding and cytology of sugar cane. IV. The origin of the increase of chromosome number in species hybrids of *Saccharum*. *Euphytica* 10: 325-342.

Bunting A. H. (1971) Productivity and profit, or is your vegetative phase really necessary. *Annals of Applied Biology* 67: 265-272.

Burns W. (1946) Corm and bulb formation in plants with special reference to the Gramineae. *Transactions of the Botanical Society of Edinburgh* 34: 316-347.

Chaloner W. G. (1984) Plants, Animals and Time. *The Paleaobotanist* 32: 197-202.

Chang T.-T. (1976) The origin, evolution, cultivation, dissemination and diversification of Asian and African rices. *Euphytica* 25: 425-441.

Chao C. S. (1989) *A Guide to Bamboos Grown in Britain.* Royal Botanic Gardens, Kew, pp. 47.

Chapman G. P. (1971) *Patterns of change in Tropical Plants.* London University Press, pp. 112.

Chapman G. P. (ed.) (1990) *Reproductive Versatility in The Grasses.* Cambridge University Press, pp. 295

Chapman G. P. (1992a) Apomixis and Evolution. In: Chapman G. P. (ed.) *Grass Evolution and Domestication.* Cambridge University Press, pp. 138-155.

Chapman G. P. (1992b) Domestication and its changing agenda. In: Chapman G. P. (ed.) *Grass Evolution and Domestication.* Cambridge University Press, pp. 316-337.

Clapham A. R., Tutin T. G. and Warburg E. F. (1952) *Flora of the British Isles.* Cambridge University Press, pp. 1591.

Clapham A. R., Tutin T. G. and Moore D. M. (1987) *Flora of the British Isles.* Third edition. Cambridge University Press, pp. 688.

Clark L. G. and Fisher J. B. (1987) Vegetative morphology of grasses: shoots and roots. In: Söderstrom, T. R. et al. (eds) *Grass: Systematics and Evolution.* Smithsonian Institution Press, Washington, pp. 37-45.

Clayton W. D. (1990) The Spikelet. In: Chapman G. P. (ed.) *Reproductive Versatility in The Grasses.* Cambridge University Press, pp. 32-51.

Clayton W. D. and Renvoize S. A. (1986) *Genera Graminum: Grasses of the World.* Kew Bulletin Additional Series 13. HMSO, London, pp. 389.

Clayton W. D. and Renvoize S. A. (1992) A system of classification for the grasses. In: Chapman G. P. (ed.) *Grass Evolution and Domestication.* Cambridge University Press, pp. 338-353.

Connor H. E. (1979) Breeding systems in grasses: a survey. *New Zealand Journal of Botany* 17: 547-574.

Coombs J. (1985) Carbon metabolism. In: Coombs J., Hall D. O., Long S. P. and Scurlock J. M. O. (eds) *Techniques in Bioproductivity and Photosynthesis.* Pergamon Press, Oxford, pp. 139-157.

Davies M. S. and Hillman G. C. (1992) Domestication of cereals. In: Chapman G. P. (ed.) *Grass Evolution and Domestication.* Cambridge University Press, pp. 199-224.

de Wet J. M. S. (1992) The three phases of cereal domestication. In: Chapman G. P. (ed.) *Grass Evolution and Domestication.* Cambridge University Press, pp. 176-198.

Dhaliwal H. S. and King P. J. (1978) Direct pollination of *Zea mays* ovules in vitro with *Zea mays, Zea mexicana* and *Sorghum bicolor* pollen. *Theoretical and Applied Genetics* 53: 43-46.

Donald C. M. (1968) The Breeding of Crop Ideotypes. *Euphytica* 17: 388-403.

Edwards G. E. and Huber S. C. (1981) The $C_4$ pathway. In: Hatch M. D. and Boardman N. K. (eds) *The Biochemistry of Plants - a Comprehensive Treatise, vol. 8.* Academic Press, New York, ch. 6.

Evans L. T. and Peacock W. J. (eds) (1981) *Wheat Science - Today and Tomorrow.* Cambridge University Press, pp. 304.

Flavell R. B., Bennett M. D., Seal A. G. and Hutchinson J. (1987) Chromosome structure and organisation. In: Lupton F. G. H. (ed.) *Wheat Breeding: its Scientific Basis.* Chapman and Hall, London, pp. 211-268.

Frodin, D. G. (1984) *Guide to Standard Floras of the World.* Cambridge University Press, pp. 619.

Galinat W. C. (1983) The origin of maize as shown by leaf morphological traits of its ancestor teosinte. *Maydica* 28: 121-138.

Goller H. (1983) Anatomie adulter Gramineenwurzeln und ihre taxonomische Verwertbarkeit. In: Böhm W., Kutschera L. and Lichtenegger E. (eds) *Root Ecology and its Practical Applications.* Verlag Gumpenstein, Irdning, Austria, pp. 43-50.

Good R. O. (1964) *The Geography of Flowering Plants.* Third edition. Longman Group UK Limited, London, pp. 518.

Gupta P. K. and Baum B. R. (1989) Stable classification and nomenclature in the Triticeae: desirability, limitations and prospects. *Euphytica* 41: 191-197.

Hanke D. E. (1990) Seeding the bamboo revolution. *Nature* 334: 291-292.

Harberd D. J. (1961) Observations on populations of *Festuca rubra. The New Phytologist* 60: 184-206.

Harberd D. J. (1962) Some observations of natural clones in *Festuca ovina. New Phytologist* 61: 85-100.

Harlan J. R. (1965) The possible role of weed races in the evolution of cultivated plants. *Euphytica* 14: 173-176.

Harlan J. R. (1992) Origins and processes of domestication. In: Chapman G. P. (ed.) *Grass Evolution and Domestication.* Cambridge University Press, pp. 159-175 .

Hattersley P. W. (1992) Significance of intra-$C_4$ photosynthetic pathway variation in grasses of arid and semi-arid regions. In: Chapman G. P. (ed.) *Desertified Grasslands, their Biology and Management.* Academic Press, London, pp. 181-212.

Hattersley P. W. and Watson L. (1992) Diversification of photosynthesis. In: Chapman
    G. P. (ed.) *Grass Evolution and Domestication*. Cambridge University Press,
    pp. 38-116.
Hattersley P. W., Wong S-C., Perry S. and Roksandic Z. (1986) Comparative ultrastruc-
    ture and gas exchange characteristics of the $C_3$-$C_4$ intermediate *Neurachne minor*
    S. T. Blake (Poaceae). *Plant, Cell and Environment* 9: 217-233.
Hay R. K. M. and Walker A. J. (1989) *An Introduction to the Physiology of Crop Yield*.
    Longman, Harlow, pp. 292.
Hayman D. L. (1992) The S-Z self-incompatibility system in the grasses. In: Chapman
    G. P. (ed.) *Grass Evolution and Domestication*. Cambridge University Press,
    pp. 117-137.
Heslop-Harrison J. (1961) Photoperiodic effects on sexuality, breeding system and seed
    germination in *Rottboelia exaltata:* Apomixis, environment and adaptation.
    *Proceedings of the 11th International Botanical Congress*, Montreal: 891-895.
Hitch P. A. and Sharman B. C. (1971) The vascular pattern of festucoid grass axes, with
    particular reference to nodal plexi. *Botanical Gazette* 132: 38-56.
Hoisington D. (1992) Maize as a model system. In: Chapman G. P. (ed.) *Grass Evolution
    and Domestication*. Cambridge University Press, pp. 266-289.
Holm L. G., Plucknett D. L., Pancho J. V. and Herberger J. P. (1977) T*he World's Worst
    Weeds, Distribution and Biology*. Univ. Press Hawaii, Honolulu, pp. 609.
Jackson B. D. (1928) *A Glossary of Botanic Terms with their Derivation and Accent*.
    Duckworth, London, pp. 481.
Janzen D. H. (1976) Why bamboos wait so long to flower. *Annual Reviews of Ecology
    and Systematics* 7: 347-91.
Jones D. F. (1934) Unisexual maize plants and their bearing on sex differentiation in other
    plants and animals. *Genetics* 19: 552-67.
Kasasian L. (1964) *Common Weeds of Trinidad*. Regional Research Centre, University of
    the West Indies, pp. 82.
Kasasian L. (1971) *Weed Control in the Tropics*. L. Hill, London, pp. 307.
Knox R. B. (1967) Apomixis, seasonal and population differences in grasses. *Science* 157:
    325-326.
Kochert G. (1992) Rice as a model system. In: Chapman G. P. (ed.) *Grass Evolution and
    Domestication*. Cambridge University Press, pp. 290-315.
Lagudah E. S. and Appels R. (1992) Wheat as a model system. In: Chapman G. P. (ed.).
    *Grass Evolution and Domestication*. Cambridge University Press, pp. 225-265.
Lupton F. G. H. (ed.) (1987) *Wheat Breeding, its Scientific Basis*. Chapman and Hall,
    London, pp. 566.
Mangelsdorf P. C., MacNeish R. S. and Galinat W. C. (1964) Domestication of corn.
    *Science* 143: 538-545.
McClure F. A. (1966) *The Bamboos: a fresh perspective*. Harvard University Press,
    Cambridge, MA., pp. 347.
Mogensen H. L. (1990) Fertilisation and early embryogenesis. In: Chapman G. P. (ed.)
    *Reproductive Versatility in the Grasses*. Cambridge University Press, pp. 76-99.
Moody K. (1991) Weed control in upland rice with emphasis on grassy weeds. In: Baker
    F. W. G. and Terry P. J. (eds) *Tropical Grassy Weeds*. CAB International,
    Wallingford, pp. 164-178.
Nadgauda R. S., Parasharami V. A. and Mascarenhas A. F. (1990) Precocious flowering
    and seeding behaviour in tissue cultured bamboos. *Nature* 334: 335-336.
Oka H. I. (1988) *Origin of Cultivated Rice*. Elsevier, Amsterdam, pp. 254.

Patrick J. W. (1972) Vascular system of the stem of the wheat plant. I. Mature state. *Australian Journal of Botany* 20: 49-63.

Prendergast H. D. V. and Hattersley P. W. (1987) Australian $C_4$ grasses (Poaceae): Leaf blade anatomical features in relation to $C_4$ acid decarboxylation types. *Australian Journal of Botany* 35: 355-382.

Rathnam C. K. M. and Chollet R. (1980) Photosynthetic carbon metabolism in $C_4$ plants and $C_3$-$C_4$ intermediate species. In: Reinhold L., Harborne J. B. and Swain T. (eds) *Progress in Phytochemistry, vol. 6.* Pergamon Press, Oxford, pp. 1-48.

Renvoize S. A. and Clayton W. D. (1992) Classification and evolution of the grasses. In: Chapman G. P. (ed.) *Grass Evolution and Domestication.* Cambridge University Press, pp. 3-37.

Renvoize S. A., Cope T. A., Cook F. E. M., Clayton W. D. and Wickens G. E. (1992) Distribution and utilisation of grasses in arid and semi-arid regions. In: Chapman G. P. (ed.) *Desertified Grasslands; their biology and management.* Academic Press, London, pp. 3-16.

Richards A. J. (1990) The implications of reproductive versatility for the structure of grass populations. In: Chapman G. P. (ed.) *Reproductive Versatility in the Grasses.* Cambridge University Press, pp. 131-153.

Robinson S. P. and Walker D. A. (1981) Photosynthetic Carbon Reduction Cycle. In: Hatch M.D. and Boardman N. K. (eds) T*he Biochemistry of Plants - a Comprehensive Treatise, vol. 8.* Academic Press, New York, pp. 194-236.

Söderstrom T. R. (1981) The grass subfamily Centothecoideae. *Taxon* 30: 614-15.

Stace C. A. (1991) *New Flora of the British Isles.* Cambridge University Press, pp. 1226.

Tomlinson P. B. (1970) Monocotyledons - Towards an understanding of their morphology and anatomy. *Advances in Botanical Research* 3: 208-292.

Turpin P. J. F. (1819) Mémoire sur l'inflorescence des Graminées et des Cypérées, comparée avec celle des autres végétaux sexifères; suivi de quelques observations sur les disques. *Mem. Mus. Hist. Nat. Paris* 4: 67.

Watson L. (1990) The grass family, Poaceae. In: Chapman G. P. (ed.) *Reproductive Versatility in the Grasses.* Cambridge University Press, pp. 1-31.

Watson L. and Dallwitz M. J. (1988) *Grass genera of the World: Interactive Identification and Information Retrieval.* Research School of Biological Sciences, Australian National University, Canberra, pp. 45.

Watson L. and Dallwitz M. J. (1992) *The Grass Genera of the World.* CAB International, Wallingford, pp. 1024.

Wegener A. (1924) T*he Origins of Continents and Oceans.* Methuen and Co., London, pp. 212.

Young B. A., Sherwood R. T. and Bashaw E. C. (1979) Cleared pistil and thick-sectioning techniques for detecting aposporous apomixis in grass. *Canadian Journal of Botany* 57: 1668-1672.

# Index